PRAISE FOR RET

T0151847

"This little book contains more wisdom about Iran than exists in the White House, Congress, the State Department, and the Pentagon combined. Anyone who wants to understand the world's most misunderstood country will find no better source."

—Stephen Kinzer, author of *All the Shah's Men: An American Coup and the Roots of Middle East Terror*

"A necessary and timely education on one of the most politically fraught and historically significant relationships of our time. I devoured these smart, insightful interviews with five important Iran scholars about the struggle between two countries that have both been our home."

—Dina Nayeri, author of *The Ungrateful Refugee: What Immigrants Never Tell You*

"Many journalists and academics have written books about Iran. But *ReTargeting Iran* fills an important gap, a book sharply critical of U.S. policy and the Iranian government. David Barsamian provides timely interviews with major analysts that set the record straight. It's a highly accessible read and a great introduction to the U.S.-Iran conflict."

—Reese Erlich, author of *The Iran Agenda Today: The Real Story Inside Iran and What's Wrong with U.S. Policy*

"*ReTargeting Iran* is not a travelogue about Iran but a facts-only objective account of where America has gone wrong, stupidly wrong—yet again—in its foreign policy, dominated by a mythical belief that Iran has an active nuclear weapons program. All one needs to know about the threat is this: as of mid-2020, the United States had no less than thirty-five military bases, manned by 65,000 soldiers, ready go to war in the nations immediately surrounding our feared adversary."

—Seymour M. Hersh, author of *Reporter: A Memoir*

PRAISE FOR TARGETING IRAN

"This slim book is heavy with historical and cultural background that doesn't often find its way into news accounts; it's a great primer on a simmering conflict."

—*Publishers Weekly*

"*Targeting Iran* feels like sitting in on a series of riveting seminars by top experts. . . . You will find profound insight into the complex Republic of Iran in a conversational and easy-to-read format. I finished the book enlightened—which is more than I can say after watching the news."

—*Feminist Review*

"Insightful, timely, and laced with rich historical perspective, *Targeting Iran* presents a bracing exploration of Iran's current place in the world, and its tangled relationship with the West. These fascinating interviews capture Iran's complexity and illuminate the morning's headlines."

—Azadeh Moaveni, author of *Lipstick Jihad: A Memoir of Growing Up Iranian in America and American in Iran*

"A valuable book in that it covers, in less than 200 pages, many of the essential questions regarding the geopolitics of the Islamic Republic and the ominous specter of a U.S. military attack on Iran."

—Fellowship of Reconciliation

"David Barsamian is widely known in progressive circles for his interviews with prominent intellectuals on a wide range of political issues. In this volume, he presents three 2007 interviews with longstanding critic of U.S. foreign policy Noam Chomsky and two Iranian-born professors of Middle East history, Ervand Abrahamian and Nahid Mozaffari, on U.S.-Iranian relations and the possibility that the U.S. government may attack Iran over its nuclear energy program or on some other grounds. Barsamian and his interlocutors aim to provide critical background omitted from the U.S. media when policy towards Iran is discussed, such as the decades-long support for the hated dictatorship of Shah Reza Pahlevi, and [seek] to introduce a more nuanced picture of Iranian society than is typically understood by the average American."

—*Book News*

RETARGETING IRAN

RETARGETING IRAN

DAVID BARSAMIAN

with TRITA PARSI, ERVAND ABRAHAMIAN,

NOAM CHOMSKY, AZADEH MOAVENI,

and NADER HASHEMI

CITY LIGHTS BOOKS | Open Media Series

Cover design by Victor Mingovits

Open Media Series Editor: Greg Ruggiero

ISBN: 978-0-872-86804-5

Library of Congress Cataloging-in-Publication Data

Names: Barsamian, David, author. | Parsi, Trita, author. | Abrahamian,
    Ervand, 1940– author. | Chomsky, Noam, author. | Moaveni, Azadeh, 1976–
    author. | Hashemi, Nader, 1966– author.
Title: ReTargeting Iran / David Barsamian ; with Trita Parsi, Ervand
    Ambrahamian, Noam Chomsky, Azadeh Moaveni, Nader Hashemi.
Description: San Francisco : City Lights Books, [2020] | Series: Open Media
    series
Identifiers: LCCN 2020009229 | ISBN 9780872868045 (trade paperback)
Subjects: LCSH: Trump, Donald, 1946– | Nuclear nonproliferation—Iran. |
    Nuclear nonproliferation—International cooperation. | United
    States—Foreign relations—Iran. | Iran—Foreign relations—United
    States. | United States—Foreign relations—1945–1989. | United
    States—Foreign relations—1989– | Iran—Politics and
    government—1979–1997. | Iran—Politics and government—1997– |
    Iran—Social conditions—1997–
Classification: LCC E183.8.I55 B377 2020 | DDC 327.7305509/051—dc23
LC record available at https://lccn.loc.gov/2020009229

City Lights Books are published at the City Lights Bookstore
261 Columbus Avenue, San Francisco, CA 94133
www.citylights.com

CONTENTS

ACKNOWLEDGMENTS

My gratitude to the five expert contributors to this book. In addition, I would like to thank Sophie Siebert, Joe Richey, the Center for Middle East Studies at the University of Denver, and Open Media Series/City Lights Editor Greg Ruggiero, who conceived this book.

—David Barsamian

INTRODUCTION

*"One of the delightful things about Americans is
that they have absolutely no historical memory."*

—*Zhou Enlai*

I WAS SHAVING when the doorbell rang. It was 8:00 a.m.,
August 20, 2019.

When my wife opened the door, she thought the two men
who were standing there, Carlos Medina and Brian Palmer, were
Jehovah's Witnesses. But they weren't. They were FBI agents.

The two had been sent to my home to investigate a trip I
had taken to Iran years before. They informed me that they
were there to encourage me to "share" with them whom I
had met, where I had gone, and why.

"We're interested in your story," they said, because
the Iranian government "targets" people in attempts to
"manipulate" them. I refused to answer their questions and

1

informed them only that their visit was a form of harass-ment. After a few minutes, they left.

I was not surprised to get a visit. I wondered why it had taken so long for the institution that had given us COINTELPRO to drop by. Decades of associations with insurgent scholars, activists, and intellectuals did not bring Big Brother to my door. But going to Iran did. For years following my trip there in 2016, I was repeatedly stopped at U.S. airports and held for secondary screenings. In each of these instances, I was interrogated only about Iran. The same questions were repeated every time: *Whom did you meet? Where did you go? Why did you go there?* If they lis-tened to anything I told them, they know that I've long been interested in Iranian culture and peaceful relations between the United States and Iran. They also know that I intend to pursue my work here in the U.S. and in Iran, no matter who comes knocking at my door.

This book, a follow-up to my 2007 work, *Targeting Iran*, is an expression of those interests and intentions. It gives voice to five prominent scholars—Trita Parsi, Ervand Abrahamian, Noam Chomsky, Azadeh Moaveni, and Nader Hashemi—who are dedicated to educating the pub-lic about the consequences of U.S. foreign policy and why diplomacy, not escalation, should be the primary method for resolving conflicts.

Much has happened in the decade since *Targeting Iran* was published. Among the most significant developments has been the Iran Deal—also known as the Joint Comprehensive Plan of Action, or JCPOA—which took effect on January 1, 2016. Regarded as a major diplomatic breakthrough, the accord was signed by the five permanent members of the Security Council and the European Union. The Vienna-based U.N. International Atomic Energy Agency took charge of inspecting Iranian sites. In May 2018, the agency's director general at the time, Yukiya Amano, said that Iran was "subject to the world's most robust verification regime" and added, "I can state Iran is implementing its nuclear-related commitments." That same month, the Trump regime unilaterally pulled out of the accord.

What a difference a year can make. By 2020, it was almost impossible to keep up with how quickly relations between Iran and the United States were deteriorating. The year began with a game changer of a day. On January 2, the United States assassinated Qassem Soleimani—a prominent Iranian general often described as the second most powerful man in Iran—outside Baghdad International Airport. President Trump took credit for the killing Soleimani, who was the head of the Islamic Revolutionary Guards Corps (IRGC) Quds Force, notifying the U.N. Security Council of his unilateral action on January 8, 2020. Also assassinated were Abu Mahdi al-Muhandis, a top Iraqi militia leader, and eight others. The killings, a blatant violation of Iraqi sovereignty, precipitated an acute crisis and the threat of a major war. In a simultaneous drone strike against high-level operatives in Yemen, Team Trump took the life of an additional Iranian officer the same day they killed Soleimani.

Iran responded by launching a missile attack against a U.S. military base in neighboring Iraq. Tehran also announced that it was resuming uranium production, a provocative step that suggested the regime was reviving its program to develop nuclear weapons. The international diplomatic community was dismayed by these developments. As an armada of U.S. warships positioned itself off Iran's coast, Iranian Foreign Minister Javad Zarif announced on Twitter that "there will no longer be any restriction on number of centrifuges." He added, "This step is within JCPOA and all five steps are reversible upon effective implementation of reciprocal obligations."

Then the novel corona virus silently arrived, hitting Iran harder than most countries. The impact of U.S. economic sanctions crippled Iran's ability to respond to the public health emergency. Preventable human suffering and death increased. By the time you read this, the numbers of fatalities due to Covid-19 in Iran will be staggering. The people of both nations, the United States and Iran, will have suffered greatly, and the world will be a different place. When the world recovers, the work of repairing U.S.-Iran relations will be waiting for us. The purpose of this book is to inform the public why such work is so important.

In addition to addressing the political history between the United States and Iran, the cultural differences, and the evolving role of women in Iranian society, a central theme explored in *ReTargeting Iran* is the question of why Washington abandoned the nuclear deal with Tehran. Internal political conflicts are also explained—how a beleaguered authoritarian regime in Iran responds to security threats, both domestically and in regional foreign policy, and its relations with the United States. In these conversations, Trita Parsi, Ervand Abrahamian, Noam Chomsky, Azadeh Moaveni, and Nader Hashemi provide you with insights into the complexities that animate relations between the two countries. Their views and knowledge provide important insights into the millennia-old civilization and decades-old Islamic Republic.

David Barsamian
May 5, 2020

1

THE IRAN DEAL

Trita Parsi

PART ONE
October 4, 2017

Trita Parsi wrote his doctoral thesis on Israeli-Iranian relations at Johns Hopkins University School of Advanced International Studies. He co-founded and served as president of the National Iranian American Council, and is the co-founder and Executive Vice President of the Quincy Institute for Responsible Statecraft. Parsi is the author of *Treacherous Alliance: The Secret Dealings of Iran, Israel and the United States*, *A Single Roll of the Dice*, and *Losing an Enemy: Obama, Iran and the Triumph of Diplomacy*.

The Joint Comprehensive Plan of Action (JCPOA) is the nuclear deal with Iran and the five permanent members of the United Nations Security Council (China, France, Russia, United Kingdom, United States) and the European Union. It was signed in Vienna in July 2015 and took effect in 2016. The 1970 Non-Proliferation Treaty (NPT), had allowed inspections of all signatories by the International Atomic Energy Agency (IAEA). U.S. Ambassador to the U.N. Nikki Haley was in Vienna in late August 2017 apparently pushing the IAEA about the inspections and U.S. "concerns about ensuring Iran strictly adheres to its obligations."

You're putting your finger on something that is really important. First of all, the Iranians were in compliance. There were eight reports by the IAEA, which had been tasked to oversee the implementation of the deal. They were the referee on matters of violation. Eight times in a row they certified that the Iranians were in compliance with the terms of the agreement, and in some cases actually went further than what was required.

From the moment Trump took office, he sought ways to kill Obama's deal with Tehran. And while Trump may have preferred just walking out, other people in his administration proposed the same goal—kill the deal—but a different approach to getting that done.

One of those approaches was to use a mechanism within the deal by which one can request access for the inspectors to visit non-nuclear sites inside Iran. This mechanism was put in place in order to make sure that if the Iranians were suspected of doing things forbidden in the deal at secret locations, the IAEA could go there and look. What was required for such an inspection, however, was credible evidence. If the IAEA didn't have credible evidence but was pushed into doing such inspections anyway, and no violations were found, the credibility of the IAEA would be degraded.

The Trump administration's initial calculation was that if they strong-armed the IAEA to request access to Iranian sites when there wasn't evidence suggesting something fishy was going on, the Iranians would say no. Once the Iranians say no, Team Trump could say that the Iranians were in violation and blame the collapse of the deal on Tehran. Nikki Haley took this scheme to the IAEA in Vienna. She got a very firm response from the IAEA saying that they had no reason to do this, since they had no new evidence. As a result, Trump's plan failed.

Defense Secretary Mattis said the deal was "in our best interests," and apparently Secretary of State Tillerson, National Security Advisor McMaster, and scores of disarmament experts said it was a good agreement.

Without a doubt.

I was in a unique position throughout these negotiations because I was advising the Obama administration and I also had access to the Iranians. I would be at the White House early in the week, and at the end of the week I would have a two-hour private session with the Iranian foreign minister. It gave me a chance to understand both sides' perspectives—their calculations, fears, tactics, and strategies.

I also interacted a lot with the scientific community as part of the research for the deal. Within the scientific community the value of this deal was as established as climate change is. Questioning the deal on a scientific basis is as silly as it is to question whether climate change exists. This is not a scientific question; this is a political question. The science of this is absolutely solid: The Iranians essentially had no path to a nuclear bomb as long as the deal survived. This was the toughest inspections regime that had ever been put into place.

Incidentally, part of the reason the science was so much part of this was because Obama's secretary of energy, Ernest Moniz, was a lead negotiator. Moniz was a nuclear physicist from Massachusetts Institute of Technology (MIT). His counterpart on the Iranian side was another MIT Ph.D., Ali Akbar Salehi. They were actually at MIT at the same time, both of them studying nuclear physics. Whenever the U.S.

tested a model or made a proposal to the Iranians and the Iranians made some revisions to it, the U.S. side would take that revised version back to the scientific community to test whether there was a way for the Iranians to cheat if it were to be done that way. After everything was solid in terms of the science and verification, the U.S side then approved the plan.

Israel, India, and Pakistan have nuclear weapons and ballistic missile delivery systems, but none of these countries is a signatory to the NPT. Is there a double standard for Israel, India, and Pakistan? Is Iran being held to a different set of criteria?

In many ways, yes. Obviously, all of this happens in a political context. In this specific case, Israel was the main force driving the Iran Deal to the top of the international agenda, even though Israel has nuclear weapons and is not an NPT signatory.

During the JCPOA negotiations, it was critical for the Iranians to make sure that there would be a deal that would not just punish them for noncompliance, but would also reward them for compliance by giving them a path to once again be a full NPT partner, a signatory. Within the NPT there are countries that have weapons and there are countries that don't. Then there are countries—Israel, Pakistan, India, and North Korea, for example—that have nuclear weapons but are not within the NPT.

Having a path to join the NPT was essential to Iran, because some on the Western side wanted punishment for violating JCPOA to be permanent. This was absolutely unacceptable to the Iranians. That's why certain aspects of the restrictions on Iran were going to be lifted on year ten and others on year fifteen, assuming that the Iranians had lived up to the deal by those points in time, meaning that they restored international confidence that their nuclear program was solely for peaceful purposes. Once that confidence was gained, Iran would be no different from Sweden, Belgium, or Japan in terms of how they use nuclear energy.

But there were some who were pushing to make sure that Iranian nuclear energy programs were never fully normalized. Benjamin Netanyahu, for example, was insisting that there should be no "sunset," as he called it, on some restrictions that would be lifted once the Iranians lived up to their side of the deal. Going that route would turn Iran into a fourth-category nation, the only country that would be part of the NPT, but not enjoy the rights of the NPT.

Netanyahu, the Israeli prime minister, has said, "It's 1938, and Iran is Germany."

Netanyahu has, more than any Israeli leader in the last twenty years, pushed to define Iran as an existential threat.

His calculation was that he would eliminate the possibility that the U.S. would just contain the Iranian nuclear program—the status quo option—and kick the can down the road and let it be the headache of a future administration. Netanyahu thought that by eliminating such an option, he would force the U.S. to take military action, particularly since the Israelis were constantly pushing to make sure that there could not be any compromise on the issue of Iran developing nuclear weapons.

But, in a bizarre way, the JCPOA came about not *in spite* of Netanyahu, but *because* of Netanyahu. He thought that he could force the U.S. to take military action, but he underestimated Obama and he misread the American public, which has been adamantly against another war. Israeli hawks like Netanyahu actually pushed Obama into the diplomatic direction. Had Netanyahu not done this, had he not lobbied against the status quo option, I'm personally convinced that President Obama would not have made that immense and very costly and very risky investment in going down that over two-year-long diplomatic path with the Iranians.

The American Israel Public Affairs Committee, AIPAC, is one of the most powerful and well-funded lobbies in the U.S. What kind of influence does the Israeli lobby have on U.S. policy toward Iran?

The influence of the right-wing Israeli lobby, meaning groups that tend to be very close to the Likud's view—AIPAC, of course, is the leading one—is quite powerful. But I would say that over the course of the last ten years, while still powerful, their position of dominance has diminished significantly. In the summer of 2015 they spent between $20 million and $40 million.

On ads denouncing the deal with Iran?

On ads and many other things. Not only did they not get what they wanted, they ended up getting fewer Democrats on their side at the end of the process than they had in the beginning of the process. Lobby groups are able to dominate the political process as long as the American public is absent. But once you have mass mobilization by the American public, which only can happen on very few issues and in very specific moments, when large numbers of people focus on something important, then we see that foreign lobby groups have diminished effect and lose influence.

I think that's what we saw in August 2013 when there was a vote on whether to authorize military force against Syria. There was mass mobilization to push back against Congress authorizing military force in Syria. AIPAC lobbied in favor of military action. The defense industry lobbied in favor of military action. President Obama lobbied in favor of military action. Yet most members of Congress said that they got ninety-seven phone calls against military action to every three in favor. The same thing happened during the summer of 2015. The calls against the deal were larger in number, but the calls in favor were so numerous that it was sufficient for Congress to approve.

Official explanations about the deal and how it evolved are that the sanctions were hurting Iran, Tehran was desperate to get them lifted, and that's what brought them to the negotiating table. You say that Obama made a diplomatic move that was quite dramatic. Explain what happened.

Washington's narrative that sanctions brought the Iranians to the table is simply not true. And it's very dangerous for us to allow ourselves to be lulled into believing that. It presents a false understanding of what made the deal work, and then we will apply incorrect and false models on future cases, such as with North Korea. In order to understand what went right, we have to be honest with ourselves. When you see what happened in the secret negotiations in Oman that no one knew about at the time, you see a very different picture.

In January 2012, Secretary of Defense Leon Panetta publicly said that Iran had the capability to build a nuclear weapon within twelve months. In January 2013, the U.S. imposed sanctions and the Iranians responded by deliberately doubling down on their nuclear program. As a result, a new sense of urgency dawned in the White House, and they began saying that Iran had the capability to build a nuclear weapon within eight to twelve weeks.

The question then became, which clock would tick faster, the sanctions clock or the nuclear clock? Would the U.S. be able to sufficiently cripple the Iranian economy before Tehran could present the U.S. with a nuclear fait accompli?

By January 2013 the president understood that if nothing else changed, the U.S. would be faced with only two options: either accept that Iran would becoming a de facto nuclear power, or attack. The U.S. chose the diplomatic route, which Obama had planned to do at the end of the negotiation, not in the beginning of the negotiation. He went to the Iranians and said, "We accept your red line. We accept that you can have nuclear enrichment on your soil." This was the absolute red line of the Iranians. They would never compromise on this, regardless of how much pressure and how many sanctions were put on them.

In March 2013, Mahmoud Ahmadinejad was still president of Iran. Obama sent a senior delegation of diplomats to go to Oman. This would be the second meeting. The first meeting, in July 2012, did not go well. But this time around

Obama sent a senior delegation, including the number two official at the State Department, Ambassador William Burns. For the very first time, he allowed the U.S. diplomats to have an instrument in their hands that they were not allowed to have before: a carefully worded statement on how, when, and under what circumstances the U.S. would be willing to concede to the Iranians on the issue of nuclear enrichment. This happened during the Ahmadinejad years, and led to the breakthrough in the negotiations. Had this concession not been made, there never would have been a deal. And in reverse, if this concession had been made ten years earlier, there would have been an even better deal for the U.S., because during that period the Iranians *were* advancing their nuclear weapons program.

That goes back to the whole context of U.S.-Iranian relations, which have been more than murky since the overthrow of the shah in 1978–79 and the introduction of the Islamic regime of Ayatollah Khomeini. That relationship, once very close, became quickly estranged.

The history of the U.S. and Iran is a rather sad one over the last several decades. The list of offenses committed by both sides is very long. One of the main achievements of the JCPOA was the recognition that they can't sort out the past but they can sort out the future. And they were willing to set aside some past grievances to ensure that there wouldn't be new grievances coming up, or at least there would be fewer.

That's why my book is called *Losing an Enemy*. I'm not making the argument that the U.S. lost an enemy; I'm making the argument that there was an opportunity to lose an enemy, an opportunity that had to be embraced and built upon. An opportunity that now has been squandered by the Trump administration. This is quite sad, because we have to ask ourselves, when was the last time the U.S. lost an enemy in the Middle East?

Neoconservatives and others point to the Friday post-prayer chanting of "Death to America" and "Death to Israel" as evidence of Iran's deep enmity toward both countries. Why is the Iranian leadership, or at least parts of it, so focused on Israel?

The focus on Israel has been a central part of the Iranian strategy to come across as a Pan-Islamic power and to create a wedge between the pro-American Arab regimes and the people on the "Arab street." But as much as Iran has invested in this, it has lost much of its potency in the post–Arab Spring. We have seen less and less of it.

At the U.N. in September 2017, President Trump called the Iran Deal "an embarrassment to the U.S." and "one of the worst and most one-sided transactions the U.S. has ever entered into." He also said that under the deal the U.S. gave Iran $150 billion and got nothing in return.

That was completely false. There was no $150 billion from the U.S. that went to the Iranians. Part of the sanctions regime froze funds that Iran held in foreign banks, primarily in Switzerland, Japan, elsewhere. These were funds used to pay for imports from those countries. As part of the deal, the Iranians regained access to those funds. It was Iran's own money. It wasn't U.S. money.

There was a much smaller amount of money, roughly $1.7 billion, that was transferred as the result of an Iranian lawsuit against the United States. The Iranians were purchasing fighter jets from the U.S. during the last years of the shah. The shah's government had paid the United States. But when the shah was deposed and the Iranians took fifty-two American diplomats hostage, the U.S. did not give the money back, nor did it send the airplanes to Iran.

The Iranians took the U.S. to the International Court, and it was very clear the U.S. would have lost. The original sum was $400 million, but with interest it would be more. The U.S. decided to negotiate an agreement with the Iranians rather than letting the legal procedures continue. Had they let the legal procedures continue, it would probably have led to $5 billion or $6 billion. Instead they settled for $1.7 billion. President Obama announced this on the same day that the nuclear deal was implemented. It didn't make much news.

Six months later, when the *Wall Street Journal* found out that the money had been sent to Iran in cash on airplanes, it became major news. There was nothing new in the story except that it was hand-delivered in cash. U.S. sanctions had made it very difficult for any bank to agree to transfer that amount of money to the Iranians, so the U.S. itself was forced to make a cash payment.

The notion that the United States "gave Iran $150 billion and got nothing in return" was one of many falsehoods perpetrated about the deal during that summer. Some were spread by Trump himself. And he has continued to peddle those lies.

The New York Times *reported that "Mr. Rouhani [the president of Iran], a moderate, has staked his reputation on sealing the nuclear deal and relieving the Iranian economy of debilitating international sanctions." How much political capital did Rouhani invest in the success of the deal?*

He underwent a lot of criticism that he had neglected other issues at the expense of the nuclear deal. But he recognized that this was such an important agreement, such an important challenge, [because without addressing it], many other problems would persist. In order to decrease the level of Iran's isolation, this issue needed to be resolved. But it needed to be resolved in a way that Rouhani could also defend at home. This was quite essential for him.

September 8, 2019

Trump pulled out of the JCPOA in May 2018. Kim Darroch, the U.K. ambassador to the U.S., called Trump's move "an act of diplomatic vandalism." Washington has since imposed increasingly harsh sanctions. Can Europe be a factor in reconfiguring a deal, or is it too divided itself?

Europe can do much more; perhaps it can even save the deal. But it would require a degree of political will that does not appear to currently exist in a Europe plagued by a variety of crises.

Tehran has a maximum patience strategy as a counterpoint to Washington's maximum pressure campaign. Iran will wait out Trump and hope he is replaced. Talk about the danger of that not happening or of a new president being even more bellicose. The latter is hard to imagine, but it is possible.

War is definitely a risk. Since the European Union has done nothing concrete to save the nuclear deal, Iran does not believe it should unilaterally remain in an agreement that the other signatories are no longer are adhering to. As this process continues, the risk of war increases accordingly.

How are people in Iran coping with the deprivations caused by the sanctions? Does resisting the U.S. become a matter of pride?

The Iranian people are suffering tremendously under sanctions imposed by the United States. They have been here before, and in the past Tehran has not capitulated, but escalated. That is what we are seeing today as well.

How would you assess Rouhani's position?

Not surprisingly, Rouhani's position has been weakened by Trump's diplomatic vandalism. But it goes deeper than that. The very idea that diplomacy with the West can benefit Iran has taken a severe beating as a result of Washington's duplicity under Trump and Europe's weakness.

In terms of the political structures in Iran, one often hears the terms "hard-liner" and "reformer." What do these terms mean in the Iranian context? Who's who here?

Rouhani was never a reformist; he was a centrist and a prag-
matist. He was much closer to Akbar Hashemi Rafsanjani
[prime minister from 1989 to 1997 and a founding member of the Islamic Republic]. Back in the late 1990s, he was
on the opposite side of the reformist president, Mohammad
Khatami. But over the years Khatami and Rafsanjani managed to spearhead an effort to create an alliance between the
pragmatists and the reformists, even though they had been
at odds with each other twenty years earlier. That coali-
tion led to Rouhani's electoral victory. Rouhani would not
have won without the reformist votes—the people who were
out in the streets only four years earlier supporting [former
prime minister] Mousavi and [Shia cleric] Karroubi and the
Green Movement. That was his primary base of support.

Then you have various factions of conservatives. They
were very skeptical about the nuclear deal. Their skepticism
was not due to the terms of the deal, or even because they
were ideologically opposed to making an agreement with the
United States. All of those in Washington who were making
the argument that a deal with Iran would never work were
proven utterly wrong. That was an ideological hiccup on the
U.S. side more than on the Iranian side.

The problem for the conservatives in Iran was what might
happen in the aftermath of the deal. Would the agreement
be a stepping-stone for a larger U.S.-Iran rapprochement? If

that were the case, would the U.S. attempt to move into Iran economically and gain influence? If that were to happen, the conservatives' grip on the Iranian economy would weaken, ultimately affecting the balance of power within Iran. So their opposition was ultimately rooted in fear that an opening up of Iran to the West entirely would be very detrimental to their interests.

They are not incorrect in that analysis. I think that's precisely why the reformers want to open up Iran, because they recognize that an Iran that is more open to the outside world, that has more normal interactions, would also be an Iran in which the conservative faction would shrink.

What is the dynamic between President Rouhani and Supreme Leader Khamenei? Who holds ultimate power in the country?

Part of the reason Rouhani has been able to be a bit more effective than what a reformist president was under Khatami, and potentially other reformist presidents, is precisely because he has a different working relationship with Khamenei, and his modus operandi has not necessarily been to oppose and confront Khamenei directly but to bring him to his side. Khamenei's red line essentially has been not to betray him or the institution of the *velāyat-e faqīh*, which Rouhani has not done.

Can you explain what that is?

Velāyat-e faqīh is an Iranian concept created by Ayatollah Ruhollah Khomeini that gives the Shi'a Islamist clergy power over the state. Iran has a political system, it has a president, it has a parliament, it has a guardian council, an assembly of experts, but above all of that it has a supreme ayatollah, a grand ayatollah, who is the *velāyat-e faqīh*, the supreme leader, a religious ruler. He is the person who holds the most power in the country, more than the president—but he doesn't hold *complete* power. Thus, this is not the type of system that existed under Saddam Hussein or Qaddafi. More than anything else, Iran's supreme leader is the balancer of the system, but with his own strong tilt toward the conservative side, of course.

How would you characterize the Iranian economy today, its strength and its weaknesses? Is it a kind of state capitalist system?

This is actually one of the interesting criticisms of Rouhani by some people on the reformist side and elsewhere in Iran, which is that he's pursuing strong neoliberal reforms and changes in Iranian society, which are meeting the same type of resistance as we see to neoliberal policies elsewhere. Such policies have been effective in creating economic growth, but at the expense of massive inequality in Iran. Iran has significant inequality right now—plausibly, potentially, more than it did even during the time of the shah.

One of the main problems for the Iranian economy right now is that the sanctions relief simply hasn't worked. Rouhani needs to create a lot of jobs. The economy is growing at approximately 6.6 percent this year, but that is mainly because he's able to sell more oil compared to before, because the oil sanctions relief has worked. But to create jobs, you can't just sell oil. You have to have investments. When you only sell oil, it strengthens the state companies, not the private sector. So we've seen significant growth in Iran, but we haven't seen unemployment shrink as much.

Unemployment has further suffered from the fact that Rouhani has been very aggressive in trying to push down inflation. He got it down from roughly 40 percent to 10 percent. That is a significant achievement, but it also comes at the expense of other things, this combination of pushing down inflation and not having investments that would create jobs—because pushing down inflation tends to do the opposite. It has created a situation in which a lot of people are not terribly happy with the economy. But they are still giving Rouhani political support, because he's still seen as a better candidate, an alternative, than anyone that the conservatives have put forward.

In Pakistan, Turkey, Egypt, and other countries the military plays a major role in the economy. What about Iran?

The Islamic Revolutionary Guards Corps (IRGC) has significant economic power. They are corrupt, they operate like a mafia, and right now they are in a confrontation with Rouhani. Rouhani has arrested several of their leaders. He has done this because he recognizes that they're getting too much power, but also that it's very difficult for the Iranian economy to really pick up and get investments to come in if you have a shady oligarchy run by the military that is above the law. That needs to be dismantled in order for Iran's economy to become more transparent and more functional. The fault line between Rouhani and the IRGC is one of the biggest in Iranian politics right now.

Is the IRGC under the control of Supreme Leader Khamenei?

Ostensibly, yes. But the Iranian military is a very big institution, and much of what is happening right now is that former IRGC officials have moved into the economic sector. They have a strong network there, and they are not necessarily abiding by the rules. Again, Khamenei is a balancer. He seems to be in agreement that they have become perhaps a little bit too big and has not objected, or at least has not stood in the way of Rouhani clamping down. I don't think we should expect that Khamenei would permit a complete dismantlement of the IRGC's economic empire.

All countries have security concerns. Three of Iran's neighbors are quite unstable—Pakistan, Afghanistan, and Iraq. In June 2017, ISIS attacked the Iranian parliament and the mausoleum of Ayatollah Khomeini. What are Iran's concerns in terms of its security?

It's a great question. I think the answer might surprise you. The Iranian National Security Council has identified Iran's top security threats to be sectarianism and Salafi jihadism. The reason for this is because yes, the U.S. has a mighty military, and it can definitely take out the Iranian military, but if the U.S. were to strike Iran, you would see a massive unification of the Iranian people.

Al-Qaeda, ISIS, and other jihadi groups don't have conventional military power, but they have the power of creating division within Iranian society. Iran has ethnic minorities. Some of them have very legitimate grievances with the central government. ISIS and al-Qaeda have managed to move into areas elsewhere, where there are disgruntled groups, and Tehran has been worried about this because that type of penetration can create internal problems that are much more difficult for them to deal with.

The main perpetrators of the ISIS attack on the parliament earlier this year were Iranian Kurds. They were not outside actors. Outside actors have had very great difficulty penetrating Iran. It would not be easy for Tunisian or Chechen ISIS recruits to make their way all the way into Tehran. But an Iranian Kurd, an Iranian Baluch, or some other disgruntled person, would have far greater ability to do so.

Guess what is the second most pressing national security threat, according to the Iranian National Security Council? Climate change. Iran anticipates being severely impacted as a result of climate change, and at a very early stage. Most of the areas where food is grown in Iran—and Iran is essentially self-sufficient in food—are going to dry out very soon. They're going to be hit with massive heat waves. The Iranians don't have the technology to manage this. Ultimately, no one single country can handle the climate crisis alone. The Iranians are not only painfully aware of this, they are also aware of their lack of capacity to mitigate how things will play out in Iran as global warming intensifies.

Talk about the Trump-imposed travel ban singling out Iran and other Muslim-majority countries. Your organization has strongly opposed that.

The travel ban has nothing to do with U.S. security. It is not aimed at making America safer; it's aimed at Donald Trump giving red meat to his supporters. He promised them a Muslim ban. He is giving them a Muslim ban. And even though he has suffered significant setbacks in courts, visas for travelers to many Muslim countries, including those that were on the original ban as well as the current ban, have gone down 30 percent to 50 percent. So he's getting his Muslim ban despite what the courts have decided. That's why we are fighting not just in the courts, but in Congress as well. Ultimately, this is going to have to be prohibited by Congress itself, we believe, particularly with the constellation that we have in the U.S. Supreme Court right now.

If the ban were based on improving national security, then we would have started off with the countries a threat actually emanates from, whether because of the government there doing something or because of movements there creating something. We would have started off with Saudi Arabia, where so much of this problem has come from and where so many people who have attacked the U.S. and elsewhere have been radicalized.

The 2015 terrorist attack in San Bernardino is an example—Pakistani citizens radicalized in Saudi Arabia. Of the countries that Trump put on the Muslim ban the first time around—not a single American has been killed in a terrorist attack on U.S. soil by a citizen of any of those countries. Whereas 94.1 percent of all Americans killed in terrorist acts on U.S. soil were committed by foreign nationals of Saudi Arabia, United Arab Emirates, and Egypt. None of them are addressed in this ban.

Sudan was originally listed. It's not on the third version of the Muslim ban. Guess why? Because the UAE lobbied to get them off the Muslim ban in return for the Sudanese sending mercenaries to help the UAE fight the Houthis in Yemen.

Talk about the rivalry between Iran and Saudi Arabia. Are these two countries vying for hegemony in the Middle East? Saudi Foreign Minister Adel al-Jubeir says, "Iran remains the single main sponsor of terrorism in the world," and "it's determined to upend the order in the Middle East."

Both are strong statements that give us good insight into Saudi thinking. The first is a more accurate way to describe Saudi Arabia than it is to describe Iran. That's not to say that the Iranians have not been involved in terrorism, but there's very little of that, if any, we can point to since 2001.

The Saudi role in all of this, of course, is quite extensive, including in 9/11 itself; the redacted twenty-eight pages from the congressional investigation show that very senior Saudi officials, including the ambassador in Washington at the time, Bandar bin Sultan Al Saud, had contact with the Saudis who ended up carrying out the 9/11 attacks.

That evidence is convincing, in your view?

There is certainly something there that should have been further investigated, but the search stopped. The reason for this was political—because of the relations between the Bush administration, the Bush family, and the Saudis. Remember, Bandar's nickname was "Bandar Bush." That's how close he was to the Bush family. And members of the bin Laden family, who were in Washington, D.C., including at Georgetown University, were flown out of the United States with the help of the FBI a few days after 9/11. It's not enough to be able to say with certainty that the Saudis were involved, but it's enough to say something seems to have been there, and we should have investigated it. Instead, there was a political decision to shut down that investigation. Why was that decision made?

On the other issue, that's actually a very interesting point that Jubeir is making. He said that Iran is trying to upend the order in the region. That's a very strong misread by the Saudis, but it tells you something about what they want. The order in the region was upended in 2003. The previous order was one that the Saudis preferred. They want to go back to it. It was a dual containment. The U.S. had strong dominance in the region. It was an order that was centered on Israel, Saudi Arabia, and Egypt, and it was based on the exclusion and dual containment of Iran and Iraq.

The Iranians hated that order. They did everything they could to cause its collapse. But it wasn't the Iranians that killed it; it was the United States. Because George Bush invaded Iraq after 9/11, he thought that he could create a different order by just removing Saddam Hussein, and that order would benefit the United States. Bush succeeded in destroying the old order but he failed miserably in creating a new one. In the process, he weakened himself to the point that the U.S. has since been unable to impose a new equilibrium on the Middle East. So there is no order. The region has been in *disorder* since 2003. The Saudis are living in a dream world. They think that there is an order, the Iranians are upending it, and that the U.S. should restore it to the pre-2003 balance of power.

There are only two ways you can do that: either by making Iraq and Afghanistan splendid successes and, by that, having them continue to balance Iran the way it was prior to the 2003 war; or, if that's not possible which it clearly is not, at least not possible for the U.S.—you have to cut down Iran's influence by taking military action. That's exactly what the Saudis have wanted throughout this entire period. And now with Trump they see their chance of being able to sell this idea to a commander in chief who is clueless about the geopolitics of the region and the world.

The wars in Syria and Yemen are called proxy wars, where outside states are involved, including Iran and Saudi Arabia.

Yes, and the Saudis have essentially lost in Yemen, in Syria, in Iraq, and in Lebanon. I understand their calculation. They obviously don't want to negotiate with the Iranians right now because they're in a very significant position of weakness. That's why the Iranians have kept on reaching out to the Saudis and the Saudis have rebuffed them. And then with Trump coming in, why would they want to resolve this issue right now? Why not wait to see what Trump is willing to do? The Saudis have wanted to see how far they can push Trump toward challenging Iran, perhaps even with military force. And *then* they'd negotiate. Until they know how far they can drag and lure Trump into confronting Tehran, it's completely rational for the Saudis not to want to negotiate directly with the Iranians.

But ultimately we have to recognize that Iran cannot wish away Saudi Arabia and Saudi Arabia cannot wish away Iran. These two countries are going to have to come to some sort of an understanding. President Obama told the king of Saudi Arabia at the time, King Abdullah, that he has to find a way to share the region with the Iranians. The Saudis were deeply offended by this, because essentially what Obama was saying was, I'm not going to commit U.S. resources any longer for an all-out containment of Iran, because it not only doesn't work, it further destabilizes the region. Furthermore, at that historical juncture it was actually no longer in U.S. interests, because we had just struck a nuclear deal with Iran. Obama told the king that it would make more sense for Saudi Arabia to find a way to get along with Iran instead of hoping that the U.S. would fight Iran to the last person.

Talk about some internal Iranian issues, particularly the status of women. Many college and university graduates are women. Where do they find work? Are high government positions open to them?

The situation of women in Iran is really interesting and fascinating. Women in Iran face a tremendous number of obstacles, but they also have a tremendous amount of opportunities that they have created themselves, and their position in society is much stronger than it is in most Middle Eastern countries. For example, there are now women vice presidents in Iran. There was massive pressure on Rouhani to have women ministers in his administration. He did not nominate any, and a lot of people at the grassroots were very disappointed in him. Instead, I think he appointed two women vice presidents. The difference is, vice presidents don't need to get approved by the parliament.

But still, let me give you an example. We hear a lot about the presidential elections. What we don't hear about is local city council elections in Iran, which are very important. The city councils elect mayors. The mayors in Iran are very powerful. City council elections are actually much freer and fairer than the presidential elections. The reason for this is because there is a Guardian Council that dismisses a whole set of candidates based on mysterious Islamic credentials that are not publicly disclosed. But in the city council elections they don't have the capacity to do this. So in the last city council elections I believe women candidates took roughly three times the number of seats that they had in the previous election.

In Mashhad, which is a very conservative city—it's the hometown of the supreme leader and the hometown of the main conservative candidate who ran against Rouhani in the presidential election—the reformists took all of the seats. And there was a woman who ran on a platform of opposing patriarchy. Her slogan was "Elect more women." She won that seat.

What about the state of Iranian civil society?

One of the reasons I'm hopeful about Iran is due to its vibrant civil society. Iran has a very educated public that recognizes that the best path to getting the change that is so needed is through peaceful means, particularly the ballot box. They've already gone through a revolution. Revolutions often don't bring about that type of positive change. Particularly after seeing how the Arab Spring has fared, you really have to be quite disconnected from the realities of Iran to wish that for the people there.

I remember a very vivid scene. A few weeks after Rouhani won the election in August 2013, there was a massacre in Cairo following the Sisi military coup ousting Morsi. About a thousand people were killed in the streets of Cairo on a single day. Iranians posted to their Facebook pages pictures of Cairo on fire, with the word "Revolution" on top of the image. Then they showed a picture of Iranian women dancing in the streets after Rouhani had been elected, and over that picture it said "Evolution." It was very clear, in my mind, that this is a very sophisticated population that has understood they're faced with problems that no country should face, they're faced with problems that their government has created for them. But a peaceful, controllable, gradual path has a far higher likelihood of success than rushing toward yet another revolution.

If you were to imagine a different future between Iran and the U.S., what would that look like to you?

What I would like to see is the two sides losing each other as enemies. That does not necessarily mean that they will become great friends. I think there will be a rivalry remaining between the two sides. As long as the U.S. seeks to have a strong presence in the Middle East, it will be at odds with Iran. But that doesn't mean that it needs to be an enemy. I think it's important to eliminate this all-out enmity. Such hatred not only destabilizes the Middle East, it undermines U.S. and Iranian interests, and has a very negative effect on Iran's internal development, its ability to move toward a much more free and democratic society, driven not by any outside force but by the Iranian people themselves.

What gives you hope?

A larger and larger majority of Americans voicing their opposition to Washington's grand hegemonic strategy, which has given birth to America's endless wars. If these voices can be mobilized, perhaps the mindset behind these wars can be transformed.

2

U.S. & IRAN: FOUR DECADES OF HOSTILITY

Ervand Abrahamian

PART ONE

April 24, 2019

ERVAND ABRAHAMIAN is Distinguished Professor Emeritus of Iranian and Middle Eastern history and politics at Baruch College, City University of New York. He is the author of *Iran Between Two Revolutions*, *A History of Modern Iran*, and *The Coup: 1953, the CIA, and the Roots of Modern U.S.-Iranian Relations*.

Forty years have passed since the revolution overthrew the shah and established the Islamic Republic of Iran. In broad strokes, where do you see Iran today?

After four decades the regime has solidified in some ways. It has been able to survive mainly through dramatic economic and social reforms that began in 1980. These reforms brought many improvements in Iranians' standard of living, especially those living in the Iranian countryside. This, in turn, strengthened the regime very much.

Now Tehran is under pressure from sanctions. There are rising expectations from a highly educated middle class. With sanctions, economic issues have become more prominent, especially in the provinces, where there were protests in 2018.

The sanctions are by no means creating conditions for another revolution. The current regime still has a great deal of legitimacy and social support, which the shah's regime never had. Entrepreneurs and businessmen who have economically benefited, and who are tied to both the bazaar community and to the clerical community, also show support for the government.

And then there is the Islamic Revolutionary Guards Corps (IRGC), the new army, a new institution. When the revolution occurred, Khomeini didn't trust the shah's armed forces. Rather than disband the old army, it was relegated to the margins when Khomeini created a new branch of the military. The IRGC consisted of ideologically committed young people who had participated in the revolution, many as street kids. They became the core of the new army. That army played an important role in fighting Iraq when Saddam Hussein invaded Iran in September 1980. Today, Iran's defense forces are fully committed to the regime. This didn't exist under the old shah. He had a huge army, but he couldn't depend on it. He knew that many officers were not ideologically committed.

Donald Trump and the people around him are mistaken to think that economic pressure from the U.S. is going to unravel the Iranian system. In fact, it might even strengthen the hard-liners in Iran against moderates who believe in nego-tiating with the West. The strategy of moderates in power in Iran—including President Rouhani and Foreign Minister [Mohammad Javad] Zarif—is to wait out Trump's presi-dency, keep calm, maintain good relations with Europe, not restart the nuclear program, and maintain good relations with China and Russia. If Trump somehow maintains power through a second term and Iranian hard-liners get the upper hand, we would likely see two sides wanting a confrontation. This dynamic could easily lead to another Middle East war.

You have said that in the eyes of many Iranians, the government has legitimacy. But a large portion of the population—this is a country of eighty million people—is under the age of twenty-five. They have no memory of the revolution.

Memory is often oral history that you get from your family. Young people know that the revolution was very popular. A lot of their parents participated in it. There has also been forty years of ideological propaganda. So the new generation has grown up thinking very much as a generation of the revolution. The social differences that have emerged aren't so much between generations as they are between economic classes. People who have been university educated tend to come from more upper-class families. They also tend to be more secular and alienated from the regime. They want an opening up. Children coming from villages, working-class families, and bazaaris (merchants) are generally less alienated and more content with the regime.

Describe the structure of governance in Iran. There is the supreme leader, and there's an elected president. It's somewhat contradictory.

Iran's political system is a strange hybrid of republican democracy and Shi'a theocracy. You won't find it anywhere else. That's why their constitution is so complex. Iran's original constitution was actually drafted in Paris before Khomeini went back to Iran. Modeled on Charles de Gaulle's Fifth French Republic, it was a pure republican constitution. When Tehran clerics rewrote it, they imposed the concept of religious rule, in which the chief cleric would serve as the guide of the republic. In the West we call him the supreme leader. In Iran he's just called the leader.

In the West, Iran is often called a dictatorship, which is a misnomer. Iran's president and parliament are elected through a popular vote. The supreme leader is elected by an assembly of religious experts, and those experts are elected by a small group. But parliamentary elections and local council elections enjoy a high level of participation, especially when there is a rivalry between a conservative and a reformer. In an ordinary Iranian election you might get 70 percent to 80 percent of the electorate voting. In the United States we would be lucky to get 55 percent of the electorate voting. The leader in Iran could very well tell a U.S. president, "We will negotiate with you once you get true democracy, with electoral participation of 70 percent or more. Then we'll take you seriously."

Going back further, talk about the 1953 coup—Operation Ajax—organized by the CIA with the participation of the British MI6 intelligence service, that overthrew the government of Mohammad Mossadegh and brought the shah back to the Peacock Throne.

For Iran, 1953 is a landmark year. It's like a guillotine that comes down in Iranian history. Nothing starts moving again until 1979. For most Iranians, 1953 is the formative moment in its modern history. In the West you find there is no memory of it at all. I don't expect the average American to know about the overthrow of Mossadegh, but even top U.S. diplomats who have worked in Iran were unaware of the significance of 1953. It was like some Orwellian erasure of history.

So when the 1979 revolution ensued and students seized the U.S. embassy and took hostages, it was a complete shock. Iranians knew the story behind it. For Americans with lack of awareness of the 1953 coup, the events of 1979 seemed out of the blue. *Why are these people occupying our embassy? We've been good friends with Iran all these years. Why such ingratitude?* Americans' blind spot about U.S. covert operations in 1953 goes to the root of the conflict between the United States and Iran.

What do you mean when you refer to hard-liners, reformers, and moderates in Iran?

On the political level, hard-liners are those who are very firm about the clerical leader having tight control over policy. Reformers or moderates favor professionals, diplomats, and foreign ministry people having influence over policy.

But on intellectual issues, the hard-liners take a very narrow interpretation of Shi'a Islam. They try to legitimize their laws from traditions based on Shi'a Islam. The reformers are much more open to outside ideas, the ideas of the Enlightenment, individual rights, open trials, et cetera. Insofar as contemporary Iran is much different from seventh-century Arabia, moderates argue that Islamic laws should adapt to modern situations.

The country is 90 percent Shi'a. In terms of Iranian identity, what role does Shi'a Islam play?

There is a strange mixture between Iranian nationalism and Shi'ism. When Iran was occupied by Arab Muslims in the seventh century, many people adopted Islam, and Zoroastrianism faded. But there was tension between Iranism—people spoke Persian and their culture was Persian—and the new religion. Out of this tension, Shi'a ideologies grew in Iran. This can be seen in Ferdowsi's historical epic poem, *Shahnameh*. Written around C.E. 1,000, it tells a lot of stories from Iranian history. The poem's notion of martyrdom, as represented by the character Siyâvash, becomes very important in Shi'ism, and was already part of Iranian identity.

By 1500, when the Safavid rulers adopted Shi'ism as the official religion, approximately 90 percent of the population converted to Shi'a Islam. Through Shi'ism, the Iranian people separated themselves from the Arab world and forged their own national identity.

Iran is far and away the world's largest Shi'a country. Neighboring Iraq has a majority Shi'a population, as do Bahrain and Yemen. Lebanon has a substantial Shi'a minority. But where does Iran see itself in terms of its place in the region?

The most important thing to Tehran has been protecting Iran—defending the country after its revolution. The crises in Syria, Iraq, Yemen have brought about the ascendance of groups like the Alawis in western Syria. The Alawis would never consider themselves Shi'a. But it was politically expedient for them to make an alliance with Iran.

Similarly, [Syrian president] Assad's main concern wasn't Shi'ism, it was survival of his regime. Supporters in Assad's Alawi base were scared of the jihadists in Syria. So the alliance between Assad, the Alawis, and Iran was not based on religion or theology.

A majority of the Arab populations in Yemen and Iraq are Shi'a. But neither the Zaidis in Yemen nor the Iraqi Shi'as have seen themselves as the Iranian type of Shi'a. They were always separate. Their languages are different. Due to the U.S. invasion, many Iraqi politicians who are Shi'a have found it useful to be allied with Iran as their protector.

The most important shrines in Shi'a Islam are not in Iran but in Iraq and Syria.

Yes. Karbala and Najaf in Iraq, and the Sayyidah Zaynab shrine outside Damascus, Syria. But I don't think Iran's foreign policy is really determined by those sites. The policy goal has been to ensure that Assad survives. They use the shrines more as a pretext to get involved. Similarly, in Iraq, Iranian protection is designed to make sure that the U.S. doesn't make Iraq into a base from which it can attack Iran.

In your book The Coup *you write, "The U.S. and Iran have been locked in a deadly embrace." You compare the relationship to an "iron cage." It wasn't always that way. Jimmy Carter went to Tehran on December 31, 1977, for a lavish banquet that the shah hosted. Over a dinner toast Carter called Iran "an island of stability in one of the most troubled areas in the world." He praised the shah for his "great leadership" and noted "the respect and admiration and love which your people give to you."*

Not long after that, strikes and huge demonstrations ensued. And on January 16, 1979, just a little over a year after that banquet, the shah fled Iran and the Pahlavi monarchy ended.

When Carter was giving that speech, Ambassador William Sullivan and other embassy officials in attendance looked at each other in horror. They already saw trouble brewing in Iran. But they weren't at the point of realizing it could lead to a revolution.

Carter's banquet speech was a kind of compensation for the demonstration in Washington by the Iranian students against the shah during his official visit in November 1977. The shah complained that the Carter administration was not backing him enough; instead they were promoting human rights and liberalization. So in order to reassure the shah of U.S. support, Carter made the very flattering speech. But the speech later haunted the Carter administration because he had lauded the Iranian government's stability when the regime was already clearly unstable.

The U.S. embassy personnel who were seized by Iranians in early November 1979, igniting the 444-day hostage crisis, were released the very afternoon of Ronald Reagan's inauguration as president, giving birth to a plethora of theories about a secret deal between Tehran and Washington.

We've heard the word "collusion" a lot since 2016. During the 1980 presidential campaign, there probably was no collusion insofar as the two sides didn't sit down and draft a paper and say, "I'll be nice to you if you hold onto the hostages until after the election." I doubt there was that sort of agreement. But I do think there was a silent, tacit idea in Tehran that in order to undermine Carter, it would be best to keep the hostages until Reagan came in. This would never have been written down, but I'm sure there was a tacit understanding there.

I don't know if the secret dealings that the Reagan administration did have with Iran regarding the sale of arms were tied to the American hostages' release, because that came later. But the release made it possible for the revolutionary government to think that a Republican administration might be more pragmatic about dealing with Iran than the Carter White House had been.

The Iran-Contra scandal broke in 1986. It was characterized infamously by National Security Adviser Robert McFarlane taking two gifts to Ayatollah Khomeini: a Bible signed by Ronald Reagan and a cake.

They also sent a Saturday night special to President Rafsanjani. It was a very cynical move, because the whole time they had been pressuring the Europeans *not* to sell arms to Iran. Meanwhile, the Reagan White House made a secret deal with several different layers to it. The White House wanted money to fund Nicaraguan counterrevolutionaries—the Contras—after the U.S. Congress had outlawed doing so. So one way of getting money was to covertly sell arms to Iran, and then send the funds to the Contras. Simultaneously, the Israelis sought a rapprochement with Iran. They persuaded not Reagan himself, but people around him, that it was important to build bridges. The way they rationalized it was that there were moderates in the regime and they wanted to establish good relations with them.

In The Coup *you use the Farsi term* dast-e-panhaan, *a secret hand. Is there a current in Iranian political thinking that there are always under-the-table dealings?*

Yes. Some people would say there's a sort of a paranoid notion of history. But sometimes paranoia can be an actual reflection of reality. In the nineteenth century, Iran had a king. It was formally an independent state. But in reality, the power behind the throne was the Czarist embassy. After 1917, Britain was seen as the power behind the throne, and the reality was that Iranian government ministers basically *were* British puppets. Similarly, during the shah's reign, foreign embassies were viewed as seats of power.

This creates the context where people are always looking behind the scenes. Who is really pulling the strings? Who is really making the decisions? This line of questioning has becomes very much a part of Iran's public discourse. It often happens in societies, including the United States, where there is a wide gap between the elite and the general public. For example, following September 11, 2001, many people in the U.S. felt that the official explanation of the attacks was not accurate and shouldn't be accepted.

This kind of conspiratorial thinking goes on in Iran today. For example, there are monarchists in Iran who do not believe a revolution happened. They believe the U.S. decided the shah was no longer a useful puppet, so they threw him out and brought in a new American puppet, Khomeini.

Iraq invaded Iran in September of 1980. This had devastating effects on Iran; hundreds of thousands of people were killed, and many more wounded. And the U.S. actively joined the Iraqi side. In 1987–88 the U.S. Navy attacked Iranian oil installations. And then on July 3, 1988, the U.S. shot down a civilian plane, Iran Air flight 655, resulting in the death of 290 passengers and crew. That essentially pushed Khomeini to sue for peace with Iraq.

The war with Iraq was another formative period, especially for the generation that rules Iran now. When Saddam Hussein invaded Iran, it was clearly perceived as a foreign invasion. By international law, the international community should have come to Iran's aid. Iraq used weapons of mass destruction—poison gas—and there were no complaints from the West. There was silence. So the lesson the rulers in Iran learned was that they could not depend on the West for security.

Although the U.S. was not involved in the poison gas, the U.S. *was* complicit in it by encouraging the Arab Gulf states to give billions of dollars to Saddam Hussein's war effort. They wanted him to survive.

The war could have ended in 1982. But Khomeini believed that if he prolonged it, Shi'a in Iraq would rise up and overthrow Saddam Hussein. That didn't happen. Iranian forces weren't strong enough to conquer Iraq, and the Iraqis weren't strong enough to defeat Iran. In a stalemate, like World War I, it became clear to the Iranian elite that the only way out was to sue for peace.

Washington today says Iran is "meddling" in the Middle East by interfering in the internal affairs of the countries of the region. It's a rather interesting claim, given that the U.S. has a string of bases and occupies multiple countries in the

region. Explain why this threat hyped through the media is
so effective in convincing many people that Iran is a strate-
gic menace to the U.S. and the so-called West.

There is a strong reservoir of anti-Iranian feelings in the
United States due to the legacy of the hostage crisis. Public
hostility started there.

The current U.S. strategy is very much the same strategy
that the neo-cons used with Saddam Hussein, arguing that
Saddam Hussein is the root of all problems. Now the Islamic
Republic is the root of problems, and by getting rid of that
source, they argue, other problems in the Middle East will
dissolve. So they're even tying al-Qaeda and ISIS to the
Islamic Republic. Any problems in Iraq, Afghanistan, Syria,
and Yemen are all associated with Iran. Hamas, Houthis,
and Hezbollah are all seen by the U.S. as proxies of Iran.

Once this gets established in the public mind, it's easy
to conclude that the way to get rid of the cancer is to go
straight to Iran, take out the tumor, and then all problems will be solved. In 2019 Pompeo said, "We're willing
to negotiate with the Islamic Republic but we have twelve
conditions they have to meet." To paraphrase French prime
minister Georges Clemenceau—who said, "The good Lord
gave us only ten commandments. Woodrow Wilson gives
us fourteen"—Pompeo gave Iran twelve commandments

to observe. Among them were that Iran had to resolve the issues of Yemen, Syria, Iraq, and Afghanistan, and only then would the Trump administration negotiate a deal with Iran.

Iran's military budget is approximately $30 billion a year. That's dwarfed by the amount the U.S. spends on its military and archipelago of bases.

Iran's budget is even smaller. According to the Stockholm International Peace Research Institute, it's more like $19 billion, which is peanuts compared to Saudi Arabia's $90 billion military budget. So Iran is not much of a military power. But it's suggested in U.S. media that Iran is trying to rebuild its old empire from the Mediterranean to India.

The Iranian military is not really a formal military. The Revolutionary Guards Corps is more like the American National Guard rather than professional, hardened troops. They have little offensive capability.

What about Iran's ballistic missiles? Couldn't they be characterized as offensive weapons?

At one time they were probably experimenting with or thinking about long-range missiles. But since the nuclear deal, they haven't progressed on long-range missiles. They have short-range missiles and medium-range missiles. This is not something unique. Neighboring countries have them. The Saudis have had long-range missiles for a long time. Iran is not introducing something new.

Does Tehran see Iranian support for Palestine as a way to endear itself to the larger Arab Muslim population in the Middle East?

Because Iran is Shi'a, one way of appealing to the outside has been to be more militant about supporting the Palestinian issue. But a lot of it is rhetoric. Iran has made sure *not* to directly confront Israel. So they may talk about Palestinian rights. Sure, they have helped support Hezbollah, but Hezbollah's main concern is protecting Lebanon. And Hezbollah has never really talked about the liberation of Palestine.

Mohammad Khatami [Iranian president, 1997–2005] went on record saying that if the Palestinians were willing to settle for a two-state solution, Iran would be happy to accept that. So the idea that Iran is out to destroy Israel is absolutely wrong. You might hear anti-Israel slogans in parades and rallies, but this is just rhetorical. And, of course, Israel has often talked about the destruction of the Islamic Republic, so it's tit for tat. But I think it plays very well for the Likud Party in Israel. They repeat: *Iran is an existential threat. Iran wants to destroy us, they deny the Holocaust.* Such statements resonate strongly with the Israeli public.

People in the United States are familiar with reports that Iranians chant "Death to America" and "Death to Israel" at protests. How much of that is substantive and how much of it is theater?

It's mostly rhetoric. Part of it is ideology. That's a separate thing. But it's basically street theater. It was seen during the 1979 hostage crisis at mass demonstrations outside the American embassy when the U.S. was described as "Satan." Interestingly, the word "Satan" comes from the Persian word *shaytân.* In Iran, however, *shaytân* has a double meaning. One meaning is a devil, but the other meaning is a naughty child. During the 1979 demonstrations, effigies of Carter were often fashioned as a puppet dressed up as a little kid. So he wasn't depicted as a devil but as a troublesome child.

Reformers, moderates, and other sophisticated people in Iran actually don't like such demonstrations anymore. They are a relic from the past. But for the hard-liners, anti-Israel slogans are an important way of reconfirming their adherence to Khomeini's doctrines. Again, it's just rhetoric. When Khomeini sent trainers to Hezbollah, he instructed them not to fight with the Israelis. It was one thing to help Hezbollah. It was another thing to get into a physical confrontation with Israel. Khomeini didn't want that.

What about the treatment of minorities in Iran? In addition to a large Kurdish population, there are Arabs, Turks, Zoroastrians, Armenians, Jews, and the beleaguered Baha'i sect.

The Baha'i community has suffered the most because they're seen as heretics from Shi'ism. Many of the immigrants leaving Iran have come from the Baha'i community. The Christian and Jewish minorities haven't suffered that level of discrimination or persecution. They've preserved their religious rights—rights that are enshrined in Iran's constitution and civil law, but not in its Islamic law. They have their churches and synagogues.

With the Sunnis there is a problem. The state doesn't recognize that Sunnis are politically disadvantaged. The official line is that all Muslims are Muslims. But Iran's constitution is clearly a Shi'a constitution. As a result, Sunni Iranians can't serve as president or supreme leader, but they can be elected to local positions.

And minorities have representation in parliament. When I was in Iran I heard about an Armenian member of parliament.

The Armenians have two representatives, the Assyrians have one, and the Jews have one. The Baha'is are not recognized as a minority, so they don't have any. Some minorities get more representation than their numbers would warrant. There is very little government involvement in those elections.

What about treatment of gays and the prevalence of homophobia?

Mahmoud Ahmadinejad [president, 2005–2013] said there were no gays in Iran. He was adamant about that. There is a problem. According to strict Islam, homosexuality is not acceptable. But in practice, religious laws are not always implemented. So on the books you find strict laws against it, but in everyday life it's more of a "don't ask, don't tell" situation.

Iran has an extraordinarily rich cinema. What accounts for that?

Italy. Many Iranian filmmakers were influenced by the neo-realism of Fellini, Rossellini, de Sica and others when Italian cinema was at its height in the 1940s, 1950s, and 1960s.

Iranian filmmakers grew up in a time of intense political awareness and were in tune with the critics of the shah's regime. After the revolution, they focused on social issues.

They chose themes that were not directly critical of the regime but were covertly critical. They made social films, not documentaries. They have portrayed minority issues with characters like Afghan workers or children. They have covered the plight of women, especially around polygamy. These were clever ways of critiquing the strict interpretation of Islam. If you look at some of the old Italian movies, you can see their influence on Iranian filmmaking.

Iran is a land of great classical poets, including Rumi, Sadi, and Hafiz. What about contemporary poetry? When Ahmad Shamlu, a very popular poet, died in 2000, his funeral was attended by thousands of mourners.

Poetry is very important in Iran's popular culture and politics. Iranian poets who were critical of the regime tended to be secular, so many of them left. Shamlu was too big a figure to persecute, so he remained in Iran until he died.

There are also Islamic poets who support the regime. Khamenei, the leader, has monthly poetry readings where he participates, listens to poets, and then pontificates on which poems were good or bad. He taps into and encourages Iran's poetry-loving culture. A poet himself, Khamenei has cultivated his support of poetry to make himself look like a cultured intellectual, not just a cleric. It's a bit like U.S. presidents inviting writers and musicians to the White House for special events. But in Iran it's become routine. It's a monthly event.

What about the media in Iran? Does the government tolerate criticism?

It depends on the time. Sometimes there are openings. During the reformist Khatami period, there were many newspapers and journals that were very critical. Under Ahmadinejad there was a clampdown. Now, under Rouhani, there is a slight opening up. What can be said is always restricted, but it's not completely controlled by the state. Some newspapers reflect the reformist or moderate line, some the conservative line. It's not all in lockstep. Close reading often shows where the differences are.

What about foreign propaganda?

My suspicion is Saudi money is involved, and huge amounts of it, in financing films, videos, and documentaries that are professionally made in England. The basic idea is to undermine the Islamic Republic by creating this idea of nostalgia, that everything was so good under the old regime, the shah was such a nice guy, there was so much reform and modernization, and this was all destroyed by the Islamic Republic.

This propaganda has a direct effect. In Iran, even if the local press is controlled, many people have access to the internet, and to productions from Los Angeles, from London. Books that are published in the United States—laudatory books on the shah, for example—are quickly translated in Iran and circulated in the country.

With the exception of Israel, Iran is probably the country in the region where the U.S. is most popular.

There is often confusion between Iranians' attitudes toward the culture, citizens, and government of the United States. When it comes to U.S. government policy, there is deep suspicion. But when relating person-to-person, or to American culture at large, the average Iranian, and especially educated Iranians, are quite open. Americans who visit Iran are surprised how friendly people are. Iranians don't associate individual citizens with the U.S. state. Iranians are very sophisticated about that. Their ire is really focused on U.S. foreign policy. People in Iran enjoy Western music, pop music, and Western clothes. For Iranians these are quite acceptable. What's not acceptable is Western domination of the Iranian state.

John Bolton, before becoming one of Trump's National Security Advisors, called for regime change in Iran while

*addressing a group called Mojahedin-e-Khalq (MEK), the
People's Warriors. They've been described as a cult. Who
are they?*

Bolton and others use the term MEK to camouflage the
Mojahedin in the group's name and their Islamic identity.
A genuine radical movement against the shah, the MEK
came out of the Islamic movement. After the revolution,
the organization began to center on one person, Massoud
Rajavi, who had been in prison under the shah. Rajavi
converted the organization into his personal vehicle.
Since then, MEK hasn't been a political organization. I
would call it a cult—not a religious cult, but a personal-
ity cult. For example, at one point Rajavi vanished from
sight. The MEK didn't explain what happened to him. He
has become the hidden imam. To remain a member of the
MEK you must recognize the leader as the imam, i.e., the
infallible person who represents God on Earth until the
return of the messiah, the eventual imam to come at the
end of history.

MEK is a very small group. But it's well funded, probably
by the Saudis. They also fund people like Bolton, Gingrich,
Giuliani, who are prominent inside and outside this administration. It is surprising that some of these Washington insiders
are willing to follow the MEK view of Iran. They talk about

the Islamic Republic being gone within a year, and that the MEK would then become rulers of Iran. This line actually *helps* Tehran, because officials can then tell the Iranian public, "If you don't like us, look at who the Americans want to impose on you." The vast majority of Iranians would actually prefer the Islamic Republic to the MEK.

With Rajavi out of sight, his wife Maryam has assumed leadership of the group.

His wife became the spokesperson to relate to us mortals what Massoud Rajavi thinks. This has played into the early Shi'a mythology of the hidden imam. At one point Rajavi divorced his wife, took a new wife, and then basically ordered all MEK members to divorce their wives. After that point, if they wanted to marry someone, they needed to have his permission. This is the ultimate in cult-style control.

At another point Rajavi decided that all women are equal to men. This may sound good, but when it's done by dictate, you don't know how genuine it is. Overnight, all MEK's tank commanders were women. So you have to wonder what's really behind this organization, that suddenly you can have major cultural changes due to a dictate from the leader at the top.

Was the U.S. pullout from the Joint Comprehensive Plan of Action in May of 2018 a boon to the factions in Iran that have said the U.S. government can't be trusted?

When the negotiations were going on, the hard-liners in Iran were definitely saying that you can't trust America. And they were implicitly saying that Iran should resume its nuclear program. They didn't openly say that they wanted a nuclear bomb, but they did want the capability, if necessary. So the hard-liners in Iran were not supportive of the deal.

It was the moderates who argued that Iran didn't need a nuclear weapons program. They wanted to keep the infrastructure in place while giving assurances—not to the U.S. but to the U.N.—that Iran was *not* going to build a bomb.

When the U.S. withdrew from the deal, it fueled the hard-liners' view that the Americans can't be trusted. Privately, they were probably saying, "Let's continue with the program." Fortunately, moderates like Rouhani and Zarif still have the support of the leader to continue with the agreement, even with the U.S. withdrawal. Why? The agreement isn't just with the United States. It's with the five permanent members of the U.N. Security Council, plus Germany. They're the crucial countries. Iran needs to continue with them, because it obliges the U.N. to help Iran. The U.N. should be morally obliged to lift the sanctions and support Iran.

If the Europeans, the Russians, and the Chinese buckle under U.S pressure and stop buying oil from Iran, then the hard-liners will have the upper hand. They'll say, "Why should we have to abide by this? Let's go full speed ahead, not just with nuclear enrichment, but with the development of a weapons program." If they get to that stage, then Israel will want the program immediately destroyed, and will most likely try to push the U.S. into attacking.

What will need to happen for rapprochement between the U.S. and Iran?

The fall of Trump in 2020. But that's a big if.

February 4, 2020

Trump has repeatedly said that as part of the JCPOA the U.S. gave Iran $150 billion, "$1.8 billion in cash—in actual cash carried out in barrels and in boxes from airplanes."

Trump claims that Obama gave Iran billions. In fact, no money was given. Iranian money that had been frozen since 1980 was unfrozen. Iran, under the shah, had paid for arms that were never delivered, and the Hague International Court had ruled that the money should be returned to Iran.

In early January 2020, with tensions high, Iran shot down a Ukrainian civilian jet, killing all 176 passengers aboard. After first denying responsibility, the government admitted one of its missile batteries brought the plane down by mistake. There is a bit of tragic irony here, because Iran was a victim on July 3, 1988, when a U.S. destroyer, the USS Vincennes, shot down an Iranian Airbus civilian jetliner, Iran Air flight 655, killing all 290 aboard. George H.W.

Bush said, "I will never apologize for the United States. I don't care what the facts are." Can you talk about that case and the Ukrainian one?

The Iranian government's behavior over the shooting of the Ukrainian plane was despicable. But it was far better than the U.S. behavior over the shooting down of the Iranian airliner. The U.S. first claimed Iran shot down its own plane. Then it claimed that the plane was off course and flying down towards the U.S. ship, threatening it, thus the ship was defending itself. In fact, the plane was on its regular course, and was flying up, not down. Washington later acknowledged that the ship had fired by mistake but refused to apologize. To add insult to injury, the warship's captain and crew were given special medals for their service in the Gulf. Iran, on the other hand, admitted its disastrous mistake after three days, admitted that the military had not informed the government of what had happened, apologized, and offered an inquiry and compensation. It has also stated that those responsible will be punished. Years later, Washington paid compensation to Iran but never formally apologized.

After the Soleimani assassination, it seemed a major U.S.-Iran war would break out, but it didn't. Why not?

No war broke out after the Soleimani assassination for two reasons. Iran is in no position to fight the U.S. and is willing to wait to settle scores. The clergy in Iran have a Biblical notion of justice, i.e., an eye for an eye, a tooth for a tooth, a general for a general. The Bible has no statute of limitations on justice. And Trump doesn't want a war while campaigning for reelection. The situation will change drastically when, or if, he is reelected.

In early 2020 Iranian Foreign Minister Zarif was denied a visa to attend a U.N. meeting in New York. This is in direct violation of the 1947 U.N. HQ's agreement.

Zarif was denied a visa to attend the United Nations. This is more than a clear violation of international agreements. It means the U.N. cannot function in the United States. If the General Assembly had some guts they would move the U.N. to a more suitable place—like Bonn.

3

U.S. WAR WITH IRAN: COVERT AND OVERT

Noam Chomsky

PART ONE
May 30, 2019

NOAM CHOMSKY, by any measure, has led a most extraordinary life. In one index he is ranked as the eighth most cited person in history, right up there with Aristotle, Shakespeare, Marx, Plato, and Freud. The legendary MIT professor is a major contributor to the field of linguistics. In addition to his pioneering work in that field, he has been a leading voice for peace and social justice for many decades. Chris Hedges says he is "America's greatest intellectual," who "makes the powerful, as well as their liberal apologists, deeply uncomfortable." He is Institute Professor Emeritus in the Department of Linguistics and Philosophy at MIT and Laureate Professor of Linguistics and Haury Chair in Environment and Social Justice at the University of Arizona. Age 91 at the time of our last interview, he is still active. He is the author of scores of books.

Let's talk about Iran in the context of U.S. foreign policy following World War II. Washington laid out its Grand Area Strategy, and Iran took on enormous significance because of its oil wealth.

Oil wealth *and* strategic position. It was taken for granted in the Grand Area Strategy planning that the United States would dominate the Middle East—what Eisenhower called the "strategically most important part of the world," a material prize without any analogue.

The basic idea of the early stage of the Grand Strategy and the early stages of World War II was that the U.S. would take over what they called the Grand Area—the Western Hemisphere, the former British Empire, and the Far East. The U.S. assumed that Germany would probably win the war, so there would be two major powers, a German-based power with a lot of Eurasia, and the United States with this Grand Area. By the time it was clear that the Russians would defeat Germany, after Stalingrad and then the great tank battle in Kursk, the planning was modified. The new idea was that U.S. control of the Grand Area would extend to as much of Eurasia as possible and include Middle East oil resources.

There was a conflict over Iran right at the end of the Second World War. The Russians supported a separatist movement in the north. The British, of course, controlled it, and they wanted to maintain control. The Russians were essentially expelled. Iran was a client state and under the control of Britain. There was, however, a nationalist movement, and Iranian leader Mohammad Mossadegh led a campaign to nationalize Iranian oil.

The British, obviously, didn't want that. They tried to stop this development, but they were in their post-war straits and were unable to do it. They called in the United States, which basically took the prime role in implementing a military coup that deposed the parliamentary regime and installed the shah, who was a loyal client.

As long as the shah remained in power, Iran remained one of three pillars of U.S. control of the Middle East. The second pillar was Israel, with which the shah had very close relations. The shah's relations with Israel were not formal, because theoretically the region's Islamic states were opposed to Israel. Nevertheless, relations were extremely close, and were revealed in detail after the shah fell. The third pillar was Saudi Arabia, so there was a tacit alliance between Iran and Israel, and even more so between Israel and Saudi Arabia, under the aegis of the United States.

In 1979, the shah was overthrown. At first the U.S. considered impelling a military coup that would restore the shah's regime. That didn't work. Then came the hostage crisis [with fifty-two American citizens, including diplomats, detained in the U.S. embassy for over a year]. Shortly after, under Saddam Hussein, Iraq invaded Iran. The U.S. strongly supported Iraq's invasion of Iran, and even directly intervened to protect Iraqi shipping in the Gulf. In 1988, a U.S. missile cruiser shot down an Iranian civilian airliner in commercial air space, killing 290 people. It was a very murderous war. Saddam was using chemical weapons. The U.S. pretended not to know about it, in fact, tried to blame Iran for it. U.S. intervention pretty much convinced the Iranians, if not to capitulate, then to accept an arrangement far less than they hoped for. Eventually there was a peace agreement.

The United States, under the first Bush, immediately turned to severe threats and sanctions against Iran. The Bush administration invited Iraqi nuclear engineers to the U.S. for advanced training in nuclear weapons production, which, of course, was a serious threat to Iran.

It's ironic that when Iran was a loyal client state under the shah in the 1970s, the shah and other high Iranian officials made it very clear that they were working to develop nuclear weapons. At that time, Henry Kissinger, Donald Rumsfeld, and Dick Cheney were pressuring American universities, primarily Massachusetts Institute of Technology (MIT), to bring Iranian nuclear engineers to the U.S. for training, though, of course, they knew they were developing nuclear weapons. When Kissinger was later asked why he had supported Iranian nuclear weapons development when the shah was in power, he said, very simply, "They were an ally then."

The sanctions against Iran got harsher and more intense. There were negotiations about dealing with the Iranian nuclear programs. According to U.S. intelligence, after 2003 there was no evidence that Iran had nuclear weapons programs, but they were probably developing what's called a *nuclear capability*, which many countries have, that is, the capacity to produce nuclear weapons if the occasion arises. In 2015, the U.S and Iran finally agreed to the Joint Comprehensive Plan of Action—informally called the Iran Nuclear Deal.

Since then, according to U.S. intelligence, Iran has completely lived up to its side of the agreement. There has been no indication of any Iranian violation. Despite this, the Trump administration pulled out of the agreement and has sharply escalated U.S. sanctions against Iran. Now there is a new pretext: It's not nuclear weapons, it's that Iran is meddling in the region.

Unlike the United States.

Or every other country. In fact, what they're saying is that Iran is attempting to extend its influence in the region. Iran must become what Secretary of State Mike Pompeo has called a "normal country," like us, Israel, and others, and never try to expand its influence. Essentially, Trump has been saying to Iran: *Just capitulate*. Pompeo has said that U.S. sanctions are designed to reduce Iranian oil exports to zero, and that the U.S. has extraterritorial influence: It threatens other countries to either capitulate to U.S. sanctions or be excluded from world financial markets, which are dominated by the United States. So the U.S., as the world's leading rogue state, enforces its own unilateral decisions on others, thanks to its power. While serving as National Security Advisor, John Bolton wanted to bomb Iran. My speculation is that the Trump regime will try to keep Iran off balance and intimidated—and to intimidate others so that they don't try to interfere with U.S. sanctions.

We have absolutely zero right to impose any sanctions on Iran. None. It's taken for granted in all discussion that somehow this is legitimate. There is absolutely no basis for that. But also, the tensions can easily blow up. Anything could happen. A

U.S. ship in the Gulf could hit a mine. Some commander might say, "Okay, let's retaliate against an Iranian installation," and then an Iranian ship could shoot a missile. And you're off and running. The situation could quickly escalate and blow up.

Meanwhile, there are horrible effects all over the place, the worst is in Yemen, where our client, Saudi Arabia, with strong U.S. support—arms, intelligence—is in fact creating what the U.N. has described as "the worst humanitarian crisis in the world." What's happening is pretty clear, it's really not controversial.

If there is a confrontation with Iran, the first victim will most likely be Lebanon, which could be simply wiped out. As soon as there's any threat of war, Israel will be unwilling to face the danger of Hezbollah's missiles, which are probably scattered all around Lebanon by now. So it's very likely that the first step prior to direct conflict with Iran would be to essentially wipe out Lebanon, or something like it.

And those missiles in Lebanon are from Iran.

They come from Iran, yes.

So what is Iran's strategy in the region? You hear this term, the "Shi'a arc," referring to the Shi'a population in Iraq, Bahrain, Lebanon, and Syria.

The Shi'a arc is a Jordanian concoction. Of course, Iran, like every other power, is trying to extend its influence. It's doing this mostly in Shi'a areas, naturally. Iran is a Shiite state. In Lebanon it seems that the Shiite population is the largest of the sectarian groups. We don't have detailed records because they can't take a census—it would break down the fragile relationships that exist there in the sectarian system.

The Shiite population has a political representative, Hezbollah, which is in the Lebanese parliament. Hezbollah developed as a guerrilla force when Israel was occupying southern Lebanon after its 1982 invasion. This was in violation of U.N. orders, but Israel pretty much stayed there, in part through a proxy army. Hezbollah eventually drove Israel out. From the U.S. perspective, that turned them into a "terrorist force": You're not allowed to drive out the invading army of a client state.

Since then, Hezbollah has served Iranian interests. It has sent fighters to Syria who are a large part of the support for the Assad government. Technically, that's quite legal. Assad's regime was the recognized government. It's a rotten government, so on moral grounds you shouldn't do it. But you can't say, on legal grounds, that you shouldn't support Assad. The U.S. was openly trying to overthrow the government. That's not a secret.

Finally, it became clear that the Assad government would maintain control of Syria. There are a few pockets still left unresolved, the Kurdish areas and others, but Assad pretty much won the war, which means that Russia and Iran will have dominant roles in Syria.

In Iraq there was a Sunni dictatorship under Saddam Hussein amid a Shiite majority. The U.S. invasion destroyed the Sunni dictatorship, and the Shi'a population gained a substantial role. In effect, the U.S. invasion and occupation of Iraq handed the country over to Iran.

So, for example, when ISIS was close to conquering Iraq, it was the Shiite militias that drove them back, with Iranian support. Now they have a strong role in the government. In the U.S., this is considered Iranian meddling. But I think Iran's strategy is pretty straightforward. It's to expand Iranian influence in the region as much as possible.

As far as their military posture is concerned, I don't see any reason to question the analysis of U.S. intelligence agencies. It seems accurate. In their presentations to the U.S. Congress, they cite Iran's very low military expenditures by the standards of the region, expenditures which are dwarfed by countries such as the United Arab Emirates, Saudi Arabia, and Israel. Iran's military doctrine is essentially defensive, designed to deter an invasion long enough for diplomatic efforts to be initiated. According to U.S. intelligence, if the

Iranians have a nuclear weapons program, it would be part of their deterrent strategy.

That's the real Iranian threat. It has a deterrent strategy, what the U.S. State Department calls "successful defiance." [This is the term the State Department used in the early 1960s to explain why the U.S. cannot tolerate the Castro regime—because of its "successful defiance" of the United States.] For states that want to be free to rampage in the Middle East, deterrence is an existential threat. You don't want to be deterred. The U.S. and Israel want to be able to do what they would like, free to act forcefully in the region without any deterrent.

And it seems another component may be the threat of a good example.

There's also that. But I don't think that's true in the case of Iran. The Iran government is miserable—a threat to its own people. I think that's fair enough to say. Cuba was quite different. Looking back at declassified internal documents from the State Department in the early 1960s, there was great concern that, as Arthur Schlesinger, Kennedy's close advisor, particularly on Latin American affairs, said, the problem with Cuba is "the Castro idea of taking matters into your own hands," which has great appeal to others in the region who are suffering from the same circumstances as Cuba was under the U.S.-backed Batista regime.

That's dangerous. The idea that people have the right to take things into their own hands and separate themselves from U.S. domination is dangerous and unacceptable. That's successful defiance.

Another theme that plays out after 1945 is Washington's resistance to independent nationalism.

Yes, but that's automatic for a hegemonic power. The same was the case when Britain and France were running most of the world. The Washington Consensus doesn't tolerate independent nationalism. That was made quite explicit after the Second World War. The first concern of the U.S. was to ensure that the Western Hemisphere was totally under its control.

In February 1945, the U.S. called a hemispheric conference in Chapultepec, Mexico. The main theme of the conference was to end any kind of "economic nationalism." That was the phrase that was used. The State Department internally warned that Latin American countries were "infected"—I'm virtually quoting now—"by the idea of a new nationalism," which meant that the people of the country wanted to be the first beneficiaries of their country's resources. That would be intolerable to any empire. The first beneficiaries must be U.S.

investors. Any philosophy espousing a new nationalism must be crushed. The Chapultepec conference of 1945 warned all present that economic nationalism would not be tolerated.

There is one unmentioned exception to the rules. The United States is permitted to follow policies of economic nationalism. The U.S. poured massive government resources into what became the high-tech economy of the future: computers, the internet, and so on. U.S. economic nationalism is the usual exception. But for the others, they cannot succumb to the idea that the first beneficiaries of a country's resources should be the people of that country.

This is framed in all sorts of nice rhetoric about free markets and so on and so forth, but the meaning is quite explicit.

You recently said that any concern about the issue of Iranian weapons of mass destruction (WMD) could be resolved by heeding Iran's call to establish a WMD-free zone in the Middle East. Almost no one knows about this, because it's barely—if ever—reported in the media.

It's not a secret. And it's not just Iran's call.

The proposal for a nuclear weapons–free zone in the Middle East, and its extension to a WMD-free zone, originated from the Arab states. Egypt and others initiated that back in the early 1990s. Several such zones have been established in other parts of the world. Look at them. They are not in effect because the U.S. has not accepted them. But they're theoretically there. A WMD-free zone in the Middle East would be extremely important.

Iran and Arab states, the nonaligned countries, the G-77—by now that's about 130 countries—have all pushed for this for a long time. Europe, with the exception of England, tacitly supports it. In fact, there is almost total global support for it, adding to it an inspection regime of a kind that already exists in Iran. It would eliminate concern over nuclear weapons and weapons of mass destruction.

There's only one problem: The U.S. won't allow it. The issue comes up frequently at the review sessions of the Non-Proliferation Treaty, the most recent of which was in 2015. President Obama blocked it. And everybody knows why. If you look at the arms-control journals or professional journals, they're all quite open about it, because it's obvious. If there were such an agreement, Israel's nuclear weapons would come under international inspection. The U.S. would be compelled to formally acknowledge that Israel has nuclear weapons. Everybody knows that it does, but you're not allowed to formally acknowledge it. Why? Because under U.S. law, if you formally acknowledge it, U.S. aid to Israel would have to terminate. It would also mean that Israel's weapons would have to be inspected, not just their nuclear arms, but biological and chemical weapons as well. That's intolerable, so we can't allow that. Therefore, we can't move toward a WMD-free zone, which would end the problem.

The U.S. has shown a special commitment to this, along with Britain. When both countries were planning their invasion of Iraq, they sought desperately to find some legal cover for it so it wouldn't look like direct aggression. They appealed to a 1991 U.N. Security Council resolution that called on Saddam Hussein to end his nuclear weapons programs, which in fact he had done. But the pretext was he hadn't done it and had violated that resolution; therefore, that was supposed to give some legitimacy to the invasion.

Article 14 of the U.N. resolution commits its signers, including the U.S. and Britain, to work for a nuclear weapons–free zone in the Middle East. So the U.S. and Britain have a unique responsibility to do this. Try to find any discussion of this.

The militaristic nature of U.S. foreign policy can bring big paydays to many companies. Lee Fang, in The Intercept, reports, "Large weapons manufacturers"—like Lockheed Martin and Raytheon—"have told their investors that escalating conflict with Iran could be good for business."

I don't think it's the major factor, but it certainly is a factor. It's what's called "good for the economy" if you can produce material goods that you can sell to other countries. The U.S. is preeminent in military force. That's its real comparative advantage. Other countries can produce computers and TVs, but the United States is the largest arms exporter. Its military budget overwhelms anything in the rest of the world. It's almost as large as the rest of the world's military budgets combined. The *increase* in the U.S. military budget under Trump is greater than the *entire* Russian military budget. China is way behind. And the United States is way more technologically advanced in military hardware. So that's its comparative advantage, and I think its primary focus has been ensuring that the world remains pretty much under its control.

I think Trump's Iran policy is largely done for domestic purposes. If the Trump strategists are thinking clearly—and I assume they are—the best way to approach the 2020 election is to concoct major threats all over: immigrants from Central America coming here to commit genocide against Americans, Iran about to conquer the world, China doing this and that. And then our bold leader with the orange hair, the one person who is capable of defending us from all of these terrible threats, not like these women who won't know how to do anything, or sleepy Joe, or crazy Bernie. That's the best way to move into an election. That means maintaining tensions, but not intending to actually go to war.

November 21, 2019

What is the significance of the missile/drone attack on Saudi oil installations in mid-September 2019?

The details about the missile strike are unknown, but it's hard to doubt that Iran was involved. Why? In part it's just that, to quote the French rhyme: *Cet animal est très méchant, Quand on l'attaque, il se défend*—that animal is very wicked, just see what happens when you kick it.

Iran has been under severe attack through U.S. sanctions designed to destroy its economy so that the Iranian population will suffer enough to overthrow the regime. But Iran is a very bad animal, so it's reacting. The action was probably a demonstration of Iran's missile capabilities. If directly attacked, Iran might use these capacities to strike at the major sector of Saudi oil production in the northeast, near the Iranian border, a mostly Shiite area, also reportedly the main center for Saudi desalination facilities. That's a serious deterrent.

How does the drumbeat of negativity about Iran in U.S. media—Iran violates, Iran rejects, Iran denies, Iran refuses, et cetera—impact public opinion here?

Since Iran broke free from U.S. control in 1979 it has gained high ranking as an official enemy, just as Saddam did when he violated—or perhaps misunderstood—orders in 1990, when he invaded Kuwait. That's a fairly regular prescription for demonization. Whether particular acts are deplorable or dismissed depends on the status of the perpetrator.

There is repeated footage on TV of Iranian scientists walking around in white coats looking at cylindrical clusters of centrifuges. What are people to make of that?

Proof of their intent to launch nuclear weapons at the world. Fortunately, Obama placed an anti-ballistic-missile installation on Russia's borders to protect Europe from nonexistent Iranian nuclear weapons—and the Russians, also being "bad animals," oddly regard this as a threat to them, in violation of the Intermediate-Range Nuclear Forces (INF) treaty.

What is Israel up to vis-à-vis Iran? Would they launch a unilateral military strike?

Israel regards Iran as an existential threat. This is in large part because of Iran's deterrent capacity, which also concerns the United States. Israel's case, however, is more immediate due to the threats posed by local organizations armed by Iran. In Lebanon, Hezbollah is the prime deterrent preventing Israel from invading Lebanon again, even though smaller-scale Israeli military operations continue regularly.

Hezbollah's missile capacity is alleged to be formidable. It might someday be a retaliatory threat to Israel's periodic escalations of violence in Gaza, or some other military venture. Within Gaza, Hamas and Islamic Jihad, also armed by Iran, are regarded by Israel as serious threats, though more minor ones. But again, taking the background into consideration, the threats are basically retaliatory and deterrent. If Israel were to launch a military strike against Iran, it would probably be preceded by a massive assault against Lebanon, and now Syria, to try to prevent retaliation. The goal of such a strike would presumably be to compel the U.S. to join in and take over. I doubt that such a strike would be undertaken deliberately; the likely consequences are too grim. But tensions in the region and in the Strait of Hormuz are running so high that some incident might quickly escalate.

What are the possibilities of a regional war involving Iran?

I doubt that it would be planned, but it's easy enough to imagine scenarios in which it could develop inadvertently.

Demonstrations in Iraq have condemned Iran. Why?

One major consequence of the U.S.-U.K. invasion of Iraq, overthrowing the Sunni-dominated regime, was to sharply increase the role of the Shi'a majority and the influence of Shiite Iran. This increased further when Iran and the Iraqi Shiite militias it supports took the lead in beating back the ISIS assault that was approaching Baghdad. But while there have long been close cultural and religious contacts between Iran and Iraq's Shi'a community, the latter see themselves as primarily Iraqi. They fought with Iraq during the murderous Iran-Iraq War of the 1980s. And there is, evidently, considerable resentment of Iranian influence and control.

Why have the European signatories to the Iran Deal not challenged Washington's diktats not to buy Iranian oil or natural gas?

Fear. Europe is unwilling to move to an independent role in world affairs, perhaps along Gaullist lines. More specifically, the international financial system is pretty much controlled by the United States, and the U.S. market is of critical importance to the European economy. Defying Uncle Sam could prove very costly.

Talk about the U.S.-imposed sanctions on Iran and the fact the U.S. is the only country that imposes sanctions. Do they work? Do they work in Cuba?

The U.S. is the only country powerful enough to impose sanctions, a weapon it wields quite freely. Those who do not observe U.S. sanctions can be—and are—punished for such disobedience. Sanctions can persist for long periods, and in defiance of world opinion.

The U.S. embargo of Cuba dates back to 1960, shortly after Fidel Castro took power. The basic logic was explained by Deputy Assistant Secretary of State Lester Mallory in April 1960. He recommended that "every possible means should be undertaken promptly to weaken the economic life of Cuba [so as] to bring about hunger, desperation and [the] overthrow of the government."

The campaign reached a fever pitch under Kennedy, along with his terrorist war against Cuba. This was no laughing matter for Cuba, or for the world, when it almost led to nuclear war [during the Cuban missile crisis] in 1962. The campaign gained even greater ferocity after the collapse of the Soviet Union, which left Cuba on its knees, with no external support. Liberal Democrats took the lead in grasping the opportunity to crush Cuba's "successful defiance" of the master.

The author of the legislation to tighten the blockade, liberal Democrat Robert Torricelli, announced, "My objective is to wreak havoc in Cuba. . . . My task is to bring down Fidel Castro." Summarizing decades of U.S. terror and economic warfare, Latin America scholar Louis Pérez writes that U.S. leaders could not tolerate "Cuban refusal to submit to the United States, borne by a people still convinced that they have a right of self-determination and national sovereignty," capturing the picture straightforwardly.

The fanatic dedication to demolishing disobedience is illustrated by the activities of the Treasury Department's Office of Foreign Assets Control (OFAC), which is tasked with investigating suspicious financial transfers, a central component of the "war on terror." In April 2004, OFAC informed Congress that of its 120 employees, only four were tracking the finances of Osama bin Laden and Saddam Hussein, while almost two dozen were enforcing the embargo against Cuba. From 1990 to 2003, OFAC conducted ninety-three terrorism-related investigations that led to $9,000 in fines, and 11,000 Cuba-related investigations that led to $8 million in fines. The revelations received the silent treatment in the U.S. media. Their significance is not obscure.

The U.S. economic war against Cuba is strongly opposed throughout the world. It comes up annually at the U.N. General Assembly meetings, with virtually unanimous condemnation (apart from Israel, which loyally supports its funder and protector). In 2019 there was a departure. Brazil's Jair Bolsonaro, one of the most obscene thugs now defacing the world of political democracies, joined the U.S. and Israel in calling for the destruction of Cuba.

Do the sanctions work? It's commonly claimed that they do not. As Obama put it, when he slightly shifted course, U.S. efforts to bring democracy and freedom to Cuba have not succeeded, so we have to turn to something else. Moving from the realms of embarrassing propaganda to the real world, the economic warfare has been largely successful. It *has* "wreaked havoc" in Cuba.

Amazingly, Cuba has survived the incredible assault from the reigning superpower, but not without consequences. The warfare has sharply impeded Cuba's economic, social, and political development, as have other measures, such as robbing Cuba of its major port, stolen at gunpoint a century ago and turned into the site of the worst human rights violations in Cuba, by far.

More crucially, the assault has blocked the dreaded "domino effect" that was much feared by the Kennedy administration, the threat that successful independent development might be a "virus" that would "spread contagion," as Kissinger put it (with regard to the social democratic Allende government in Chile).

Are sanctions, as collective punishment, illegal under international law?

Not explicitly, though the collective punishment that is the explicit goal of sanctions on Cuba, Iran, Venezuela is a "war crime" under the 1949 Geneva Conventions, which has the force of international law, the U.N. Security Council has determined. Technically, the Conventions apply during a state of war, a qualification that would easily be overridden if some official enemy were perpetrating the crime.

To put the matter plainly, international law, in practice, applies to official enemies and the weak, not to the U.S. and its clients.

What needs to happen to "normalize" U.S.-Iran relations?

According to U.S. doctrine, recently reiterated by Secretary of State Mike Pompeo (who also told us that the Good Lord sent Trump to the world to save Israel from Iran), what's necessary is for Iran to become a "normal country," like his great friend, Saudi Arabia. In the real world, what is needed is for the population of the U.S. to "normalize" their own country, and matters can then proceed from there.

The assassinations of Iranian General Qassem Soleimani and Abu Mahdi al-Muhandis, a top Iraqi militia commander, and others in early January 2020 immediately raised the possibility of a wider war. Iran launched missiles on two U.S. bases in Iraq. The Pentagon reported that as a result of Iran's attacks U.S. forces sustained brain injuries to fifty soldiers, but no deaths.

There was a lot of bluster from Washington, but it did not counterattack, and the threat of war seems to have subsided, at least temporarily. Iran accidentally shot down a civilian airliner, resulting in the death of all 176 on board. Comment on the significance of what happened.

The easiest way to determine the significance is to imagine that the situation was reversed—always a useful procedure. Suppose, then, that Iran murdered the top U.S. general, the second most significant official of the U.S. government, in the Mexico City international airport, along with the highly respected commander of a major part of the army of an allied state. Would it have significance? Would discussion be limited to whether these criminal Iranian acts of war will achieve Iranian objectives? Or would the U.S. react with extreme violence, with the vigorous support of the Western world? I think that answers the question.

To be sure, such questions do not arise in a country that regards itself as the master of the universe, to which laws and civilized norms do not apply. Those assumptions are so deeply ingrained that they are virtually invisible. They are part of what Gramsci called *hegemonic common sense*. We witness manifestations daily. Thus Trump recently announced "the Greatest Deal in History," his son-in-law Jared's plan for Israel-Palestine. The announcement, with great fanfare, elicited a great deal of commentary. The essential question is: *Will it work?* Will it lead to peace and security (for Israel)? Many commentators recognized that Trump had overturned formal U.S. policy. And a few even mentioned that with this gift to the Israeli far right, as the Israeli press described it, Trump casually gave the back of his hand to international law, the World Court, the U.N. Security Council, and overwhelming international opinion. But so what?

Unasked is why we are even paying any attention to this performance. Suppose China had submitted a plan—or Russia—or anyone other than the master of the universe.

Would it have elicited more than a yawn? Or maybe a smile at the pretentiousness of a mere state in the international system?

When the plan comes from Washington, reactions are different. To paraphrase some opening words of the Bible, the Lord said, "Let there be The Plan, and there was the Plan, and the Lord saw that the Plan was good, in fact Great!" And the world obeys, quietly.

In the background we hear laments from the political class about "American decline." We only have colossal power, but not everything—a tragedy.

During the Clinton years, prominent U.S. policy intellectuals including Harvard professor of the Science of Government Samuel Huntington, recognized that the U.S. was going rogue. Huntington wrote in the main establishment journal, *Foreign Affairs*, in 1999: "While the U.S. regularly denounces various countries as 'rogue states,' in the eyes of many countries it is becoming the rogue superpower . . . the single greatest external threat to their societies."

That was before Bush's invasion of Iraq. Then it was simply asserted as fact that the U.S. "has assumed many of the very features of the 'rogue nations' against which it has . . . done battle" (Robert Tucker and David Hendrickson, *Foreign Affairs*, 2004). Others outside the U.S. mainstream might think of different words for the worst crime of the millennium, a textbook example of aggression without credible pretext, the "supreme international crime" category of Nuremberg.

Sometimes others are given a chance to express their opinions. Gallup runs regular polls of international opinion. In 2013 (the civilized Obama years), Gallup asked for the first time which country is the greatest threat to world peace. The United States won; no other country was even close. Far behind in second place was Pakistan, presumably inflated by the Indian vote. Iran—the greatest threat to world peace in U.S. discourse—was scarcely mentioned.

That was also the last time the question was asked, though there needn't have been much concern. The poll does not seem to have been reported in the United States.

Under Trump, to his credit perhaps, the veils are withdrawn. Washington openly takes pride in being the prime rogue state, which exercises its will with abandon. More accurately, Washington exercises the current whims of "the chosen one," as he modestly calls himself before an adoring crowd, while lifting his eyes to heaven.

A majority of Republicans, now in Trump's pocket in a manner with no historical precedent, regard him as the greatest of all American presidents, even surpassing Abraham Lincoln, who had some thoughts about political assassination. In 1863, the founder of the Republican Party condemned political assassination as "international outlawry," an "outrage," which "civilized nations" view with "horror" and which merits the "sternest retaliation."

The Grand Old Party has come a long way in 160 years, dragging the rest of us down with it.

Turning to the question to which we are supposed to confine ourselves, does Trump's assassinations of Soleimani and al-Muhandis pose the risk of war? The question should be formulated a little differently. The U.S. has been at war with Iran for some time. Trump's sanctions are quite openly designed to destroy the Iranian economy, imposing maximal suffering on civilians so that they will overthrow the government. Furthermore, sanctions imposed by the master of the universe apply to third parties as well; a country that tries to evade them can be expelled from the U.S.-run international financial system. The sanctions therefore amount to a blockade, an act of war.

As an aside, we may note another feature of common sense. The U.S. is alone in its ability to impose sanctions. That is a bipartisan consensus freely exercised for many years. The most extreme current case is the brutal sanctions regime against Cuba, sustained for such crimes as Cuba's prime role in beating back the attacks against Angola by apartheid South Africa, a major contribution to ending apartheid, which President Reagan defended to the end, in splendid isolation.

The Cuba sanctions have been in place for sixty years, a bipartisan enterprise. When Russian support for Cuba was withdrawn, leaving the country in dire straits, Clinton and the Democrats outflanked President Bush I from the right in making the sanctions harsher. This proceeds in defiance of unanimous votes at the U.N. General Assembly (Israel of course excepted), a minor annoyance rarely even reported. No eyebrows are raised. Another prerogative of overwhelming power.

Posing the question properly, then, *Do the assassinations make it more likely that the ongoing U.S. war will escalate, with Iranian contributions as well?* And it is a mutual affair. Unfortunately, *Cet animal est très méchant. Quand on l'attaque il se défend.* And the vicious Iranian clerical regime hardly has clean hands in the international arena.

Apart from some crazed fanatics like John Bolton and his counterparts in Iran, it seems that few on either side want a war, which could have devastating consequences. But tensions are very real, primarily caused by the global rogue state. They could easily get out of control.

Assassinations have always been in the U.S. toolbox. Was Soleimani's in any way a departure?

Very much so. During the Cold War, for example, neither side sought to assassinate leaders of the antagonist. To be sure, the analogy is misleading. It could not be done with impunity. The rules are different when the target is defenseless. It's well-known that the U.S. sought to assassinate Castro, part of the effort of the Kennedy brothers to bring "the terrors of the earth" to Cuba (Presidential Advisor Arthur Schlesinger's phrase). The U.S. also sought to assassinate Patrice Lumumba, Africa's most promising leader, but the Belgians got there first. The crime of political assassination was banned by the Ford administration in 1976.

The assassination of Soleimani and al-Muhandis (who shouldn't be overlooked—he was quite a significant figure in Iraq) revokes that principle of American law. Trump's decision, according to reports, appalled the Pentagon planners who presented it as the extreme option, assuming that it would be rejected in favor of the "middle ground," the usual practice.

As for assassination more generally, that's the norm for rogue states. Israel has specialized in it for years, as has Iran. Obama honed assassination into a high art with his murderous drone campaign targeting those alleged to have plans to harm the Master, and any other unfortunates who happened to be around.

The U.S. strategy is to turn the sanction screws tighter and tighter and imagine this will result in the collapse of the government in Tehran. Go back to the sanctions imposed on Iraq in the 1990s. Saddam's regime was actually strengthened as people turned to it for whatever crumbs they could get. Could the same scenario play out with Iran?

We know a good deal about the sanctions on Iraq—or we could know, if the constraints on bringing the "wrong" information into the public domain were relaxed. The "soft side" of the sanctions was the Oil for Food program, technically administered by the United Nations though effectively run by Clinton and his sidekick Tony Blair (referred to less politely as Clinton's poodle). The administrators of the program had extensive information on their impact on Iraqi society, more so than any other Westerners. The first two, Denis Halliday and Hans von Sponeck, were distinguished international diplomats. Both resigned in protest because they found the programs to be "genocidal." They had a devastating impact on Iraqi civilians while strengthening the tyrant. Any opposition was stilled while people had to huddle under the wings of power to survive, relying on Saddam's apparently efficient rationing system. It's not unlikely that the sanctions saved Saddam from the fate of a long string of other tyrants: among others, Somoza, Marcos, Duvalier, Ceauşescu, Suharto, all strongly supported by Washington until they became unsustainable in the face of popular fury.

The outcomes of U.S. sanctions are not unusual. The same is true of the resort to terror, though sometimes it proves successful, even short of the regular practice of over-throwing unwanted governments. Washington's war against Nicaragua is a case in point. It was condemned by the World Court, which ordered the U.S. to end its "unlawful use of force" (aka international terrorism) and pay substantial reparations. Washington responded by escalating the vio-lence and economic warfare. Finally, the exhausted popula-tion capitulated, voting for the U.S. candidate under explicit threat that refusal to do so would mean more terror and eco-nomic strangulation. The victory for democracy was hailed with euphoria here.

Hans von Sponeck wrote a very important book about the sanctions regime, *A Different Kind of War*, the most detailed and instructive account of the impact of the sanc-tions on Iraqis. But Americans have been spared knowledge of these matters. This highly important book seems to have passed without review in the U.S. or the U.K.

As George Orwell observed in his unpublished intro-duction to *Animal Farm*, in free England, and no less in its successor in world control, "Unpopular ideas can be silenced, and inconvenient facts kept dark, without any need for any official ban." Immersion in the general cul-ture, and a good education, suffice to instill the tacit understanding that "there are certain things it wouldn't do to say," or even to think.

Returning to the U.S. war against Iran, there are too many uncertainties to allow confident predictions.

The Iranians are clinging to the hope that Trump will be defeated, but who is to say a Democrat will ease up on the maximum pressure campaign?

I think most Dems—not Bernie Sanders—would keep sanctions, but not in the brutal form of Trump-Pompeo. And they'd probably go back to the JCPOA (Joint Comprehensive Plan of Action).

Frankly, I strongly suspect that Trump will carry it off, with the help of the Democrats, who insist on shooting themselves in the foot. It was obvious in advance that the impeachment farce would turn out to be a gift to Trump, just as Mueller was. The desperate effort to rig the convention to keep Sanders out, and the media campaign, which may soon approach Corbynite levels, is likely to drive away his enthusiastic supporters, the street army that the Democrats need if they are to have a chance.

And like it or not, Trump's a highly effective con man. He is a true magician who keeps his adoring crowd focused on the hand that's delivering empty promises while he stabs them in the back with the other. It's an old tradition here, but I can't think of anyone who's come close to Trump's success.

Has the U.S. left been vigorous enough in its criticism of Iranian policies? How do you separate not wanting to support Washington while at the same time critiquing Tehran?

There's no difficulty at all in criticizing U.S. policies while harshly condemning the clerical regime in Iran and its vicious practices, and supporting those who courageously resist it. We do it all the time. We should, however, take note of some curious aspects of this question, which is constantly raised, often as a stick to beat the left.

In considering moral issues, and this is one, it is quite useful to generalize. So how often have we heard the following question: "Were East European dissidents vigorous enough in their criticism of U.S. policies?" Or Iranian or Chinese dissidents?

I can't recall ever hearing the question. And it would hardly make sense. With rare exceptions, East European dissidents either ignored U.S. crimes or lavishly praised Washington—for example, when Vaclav Havel addressed a joint session of Congress and praised Washington as the "defender of freedom" to exuberant applause, a few days after troops armed and trained by Washington blew out the brains of six Latin American intellectuals, Jesuit priests, in El Salvador; they were Havel's counterparts, though analogy is unfair because the violent repression was far more extreme in U.S. domains.

But the general point is that it doesn't much matter. It's very easy to add a few straws to the mountain of condemnation of official enemies, and if dissidents elsewhere ignore U.S. crimes, it is of slight, if any, interest. That doesn't mean that we should adopt the same practice. We shouldn't. We should condemn the crimes of official enemies, and sometimes it can make a difference. But we should be aware of why and how the question is raised within the very powerful Western propaganda systems. And we should never forget the elementary moral principle that scrutinizing and condemning our own crimes is of far greater moral significance than joining the parade of condemnation of official enemies—a corollary of the principle that our attention should focus on what we can influence, typically what we ourselves are doing. Standard practice is the exact opposite, often with an impressive display of self-righteousness.

You've mentioned the U.S. concept of diplomacy is somewhat akin to how the mafia operates. Can you explain how mafia rules apply to Iran?

The Godfather decides, and that is the law. Others may mumble in annoyance, but the costs of disobedience are not slight. The mafia analogy in international affairs extends quite far. Suppose in a gangster-dominated system some small storekeeper decides not to pay protection money. The bosses don't need the money; it's barely a rounding error. But do they let him get away with it? Surely not. They send their goons to beat him to a pulp. In international affairs, it's sometimes called the domino theory: Others might follow the example. In Kissinger's rendition, the "virus" might "spread contagion"; he was specifically referring to Allende's Chile, where he warned of "the insidious model effect" of Allende's efforts to use parliamentary means to enact social reforms, which might spread the contagion to Italy, perhaps beyond. The cure is to kill the virus and "inoculate" potential victims, often by imposing brutal military dictatorships. That is a major principle of international affairs.

The domino theory is commonly ridiculed when the dominos don't fall—because the cure was successful. But though ridiculed, the principle is never abandoned, just as in the mafia. The reason is that the theory is valid.

The "insidious model" theory was not invented by George Washington, of course. King George III had the same concerns about independence for the American colonies, which might have been an "insidious model" for erosion of the empire. His concerns were shared by czarist Russia and later by the Austrian diplomat Metternich, who warned of the virus of republicanism taking root across the ocean. It is second nature for imperial powers, taken over and vigorously pursued by the U.S. as it became the world-dominant power after World War II.

Scholarship suggests that similar concerns may have been one motive for the U.S.-U.K. overthrow of the parliamentary regime in Iran in 1953, in this case concern that independence in Iran might inspire similar developments in Egypt. Such concerns surely were a factor in the launching of the torture of Cuba, in fear that its "successful defiance" of the ruler of the hemisphere might inspire others. The war against Indochina began with similar concerns, and there are many other cases.

Can the Iran deal—JCPOA—be resurrected? Should it be?

It should, but for once I agree with Trump: It should be improved. How? A major improvement would be to institute a nuclear weapons–free zone (NWFZ) in the Middle East, with an inspection regime that can be quite effective, as the record of the JCPOA reveals. That would eliminate any concern over allegations of Iran's nuclear weapons ambitions. And it shouldn't be hard to achieve. The Arab states have long been strong supporters of the idea, as has Iran. The former non-aligned countries and all others that have taken any stand also support the idea.

There is one crucial exception standing in opposition: the United States, which regularly vetoes the proposal when it comes up at the NPT [Non-Proliferation Treaty] review sessions. The most recent time the U.S. opposed was in 2015 under Obama.

The reasons are no secret. A nuclear weapons–free zone in the Middle East would require inspection and monitoring of Israel's extensive nuclear programs, and that's verboten. Worse yet, it would require the U.S. to recognize that Israel's programs exist, thus calling into operation the provisions of U.S. law (the Symington Amendment) that ban U.S. aid to countries that develop nuclear weapons outside the NPT framework. It would, in short, require the U.S. to recognize that its aid to Israel for the past almost forty years is illegal under U.S. law. That plainly won't do, so we must face the threat of major war in the Middle East.

To me, this seems to be quite an astonishing situation, as soon as the import sinks in. And the success in totally suppressing it in the context of decades of hysteria about the alleged Iranian threat is a propaganda achievement of impressive dimensions.

These are more examples of matters that would be improper to discuss, along with the fact that the U.S. has a unique responsibility to work to establish a nuclear weapons–free zone in the region. I won't go into that once again here, since the words fall on deaf ears.

4

IRANIAN SOCIAL JUSTICE STRUGGLES

Azadeh Moaveni

August 27, 2019

AZADEH MOAVENI IS a journalist, writer, and academic who has been covering the Middle East for over two decades. She started reporting in Cairo in 1999, while on a Fulbright fellowship to the American University in Cairo. For the next several years she reported from throughout the region as Middle East correspondent for *Time* magazine, based in Tehran, but also covering Lebanon, Syria, Egypt, and Iraq. She is the author of *Lipstick Jihad* and *Honeymoon in Tehran*, and co-author, with Shirin Ebadi, of *Iran Awakening*. In November 2015, she published a front-page article in the

New York Times on ISIS women defectors that was a final-ist for a Pulitzer Prize. Her writing appears in the *Guardian*, the *New York Times*, and the *London Review of Books*. She teaches journalism at NYU in London, has been a fellow at the New America Foundation, and is now Senior Gender Analyst at the International Crisis Group.

In over four decades of the Islamic Republic, what positive things has the government done for women?

It's not so much what the government has done specifically *for women* that explains the tremendous gains that women have made in the last forty years. Rather, it's changes in what the government has done for society in general, and what the government itself has come to symbolize for a very large, traditional, and fairly conservative segment of the country.

If we look at the ways in which prospects for women have shifted, we see a tremendous jump, particularly in literacy. We see a vast increase in the number of women and the diversity of women accessing higher education. We see a vast expansion of the possibilities of higher education in cities and towns, and with it, the inclusion of women at different levels of government. All of these advances have been limited and certainly need to be developed, but we have to acknowledge that inclusion of a broader array of women participating in politics has been a reality since Iran's Islamic revolution.

At the same time, the government has also curtailed women's status. The legal code around child custody, divorce, and women's status as witnesses deeply impact women. That's the paradox of the Islamic Republic for women. Rather than having this authoritarian, top-down, secular feminism that arguably only lifted up a tiny elite stratum of very Westernized women, after the revolution there was a mass expansion of women's education, far more inclusion and participation of women in public life, yet a diminishment of their legal status. Their access to public space and public facilities suffered in the opening years of the revolution, as rules for gender segregation ended up meaning women's access was separate and almost never equal.

That was the early days, when public space emerged as a ferocious battleground for various strands of the women's movement, particularly women's access to sports facilities. You can see the evolution of this struggle in women's sports today. Iran has top-performing women athletes across virtually every sphere of athletics. They are still hampered by some dress code requirements when they compete, but they are competing internationally, often with great success. This clearly shows the arc of progression from being locked out of public space in the 1980s to competing internationally in everything from martial arts to swimming and polo. Obviously the picture isn't rosy from the perspective of an eighteen-year-old competitive swimmer who has higher expectations and who chafes at the restrictions she faces. There is still great rancor that women do not have full, regular access to stadium matches, for example. But if you compare the level of Iranian women's engagement in 1979 and today, you will observe a wide and deep expansion of athleticism across social class and geographic space. I don't know of a single country in the Middle East that matches Iran in this way.

What class of women support the government?

People argue about the Islamic Republic's level of core support. How much of Iranian society enthusiastically supports the system? Fifteen percent? Thirty percent? Perhaps among a very traditional, religious-minded, and conservative sphere and those who have benefited from the various economic political opportunities that the system has afforded them. There is also a great deal of corruption in the system. So there is a clear [material] stake for that loyalty in addition to its being ideological and political loyalty.

I think the strongest core of support exists among the class most affiliated with the system. But that has evolved over the years too. You have a lot of children of mainstream officials who have a more secular outlook, and who have really benefited from their parents' or their families' ties with the system. They have a slightly different vision for the kind of country that they want to live in.

In many ways, they're more sophisticated than their parents. They are much more materialistic and seek to be cosmopolitan. They probably would like Tehran to become what Istanbul is to Turkey—a playground for modern, secular people, living awkwardly but freely atop a fairly conservative Islamic society. On the other hand, you have passive support for the system among a large stratum of the country that has many grievances and complaints but doesn't see a real alternative anywhere. These Iranians have enough to lose with any upheaval that they just plod along, aggrieved but reconciled to their lot. We have to remember that the Islamic Republic permits a healthy amount of dissent and complaint. There are constant strikes and small demonstrations over unpaid salaries, poor working conditions, banks that went bust. But when we talk about core support, this is where the system feels vulnerable. It recognizes that it hasn't delivered on its promises to bring about social justice and improve the welfare of the whole of society. Furthermore, it is more than evident that there is still a class of ostentatious rich people who live opulently, and in a manner that fundamentally affronts the aims of the Islamic revolution.

That's a really striking aspect of the Islamic Republic today. Iran's Islamic revolution was supposed to deliver social justice, but it has failed to do so. Privilege is still preserved by the few.

Iran today is much more diverse than just one traditional religious, pious class. Political changes under the system have been enormous. As a result, there is a real political spectrum, and much more than before the revolution. There are hardcore loyalists. There are also those who are ambivalent and who see a lot of flaws in the system, but don't want to see it overthrown, which I think is the vast majority. And the sentiments of the loyalists and those who are ambivalent overlap much more than people acknowledge.

Regarding education, women make up approximately 50 percent of all university graduates.

I think it's a bit more. At some point it was creeping up toward 60 percent, and then they tried to impose quotas to get it back down. That was in the late 2000s.

And over one-third of university-educated women are unemployed.

That's one of the realities that underpinned Iran's vibrant Women's Movement in the 2000s. There was a burgeoning class of educated women—the first generation of educated women in their families—going into the workforce seeking employment commensurate with their level of skill and education. But they found themselves hovering in lower management positions, never really coming up into more significant positions of influence.

That was a great frustration. It partly reflects the Iranian economy growing fairly slowly and not being very dynamic, and not attracting a lot of foreign investment. Sanctions also inhibited the startup scene, in which women have been active. But a culture of entrenched patriarchy suffuses the economy, with men in positions of power in the very companies that women try to rise up within.

That's changing a little bit in the last five years. Women are slowly coming into positions of greater influence, particularly in management. But unemployment is significant for everyone. Economies impacted by sanctions tend to affect women disproportionately. So women lose jobs first. Women's employment is most vulnerable in isolated economies like Iran's.

Patriarchy and misogyny predate the Islamic republic. But have you seen some erosion of those male-dominated sectors?

There has been some erosion there due to pressure from below—just so many more women occupying spaces, whether in universities, private companies, or even state-owned companies, pushing their way up to positions of influence in higher management. It's slow, but it's certainly happening. When you have a workforce of skilled, educated women included in the economy, it eventually creates its own pressure. It's a stark contrast to conditions Iranian women faced prior to 1979. That doesn't mean that women wouldn't have made any gains at all if there wasn't a revolution. But the increase in education of women after the revolution has been significant.

Women's bodies are a battleground in Iran—particularly around issues of hair, mandatory dress codes, and the hijab.

This is a very old fight in Iran. We can trace it through the history of the revolution and the post-revolutionary era. In the Islamic Republic today, we see different types and strains of feminism. There are activists who identify as Islamic feminists, and work to advance women's rights within the conservative and religious social framework of the country, and I underscore the country, not just the system. There have always been activists who are fiercely secular, although there hasn't been a great deal of room for them, frankly. Their worldviews and positions have been at the fringe of society, so it's hard to achieve even incremental change, which has been crucial for Iranian women, when at the core you reject the whole nature of the legal system.

Over the last decade many leading women activists have gone abroad, and the women's movement as a whole has gone quiet. Even though there has been a maturing amongst those who stayed, there is a wariness of having their causes and activism hijacked by Western governments and exiled regime-change activists who are hostile to Iran. Indeed, this is a real danger, because it classifies as a security risk a rights agenda that has traditionally been firmly focused on internal change.

Just like the #MeToo movement in the West, in Iran there are generational differences between women's attitudes toward how men and women should comport themselves and relate in the workplace, and different interpretations of what gender equality means.

In the West there is a perennial obsession with protests around the headscarf in Iran. This is the historic and almost colonial way of pressuring Iran from the outside: to invoke women and women's rights as a reason why Iran needs to be isolated, pressured, and ultimately, why Iran needs regime change.

But the sector of the women's movement that reflects my generation—women who are now in their forties, who have had children, who have experienced the challenging realities of the workforce—this sector is focused on other battles, such as efforts to improve women's legal rights around child custody, divorce, inheritance; campaigns to protect or shield women from physical harassment in public spaces; and struggles to achieve more space for activism, real women's activism. These are the issues many Iranian women are driving forward today, and which form a vibrant and dominant strain of women activists' attitudes.

Also, as Iran matures, there is similarly a maturation in how prominent, active professional women see their contribution to society. Just as in the West, some women position their work, whether in publishing or academia or art, as specifically *feminist*, while others just excel in those fields without highlighting their gender identity. The same occurs in Iran.

Certainly there is activism and civil disobedience around the headscarf. But it's magnified and complicated by the opposition outside the country, much of which is focused on regime change, and much of which is openly funded by Washington. To what extent that really reflects public sentiment among women inside the country is debatable, but it's there.

I speak to young women who are frustrated about dress codes—young women who play sports, or who are chess champions—and they chafe at these restrictions. They're frustrated that they are constrained when they go abroad to participate in soccer matches or any athletic competition.

I think Iranian society is really ready to be where Turkey is, a place where those who are secular and those who are religious are equally free. However, women's resistance to dress codes has always been weaponized by the West against Iran. This has undermined the Iranian women's movement, because it has encouraged the government and the security services to view women's activism around dress codes (and even more broadly) as a security concern.

What about divorce? Is it relatively easy for women to get a divorce? How common is it? What about child custody?

Divorce is very common. Divorce rates have certainly increased since the revolution. That was to be expected. Iran is in line with other countries that have had rapid urbanization and a rapid transformation of gender norms in the family as women are educated and go into the workforce. That said, divorce is still challenging in Iran.

Custody laws have improved somewhat. A mother had automatic custody until children reached age seven, after which custody would revert to the father. But now provisions are in place to have a court decide what is in the best interests of the child.

A woman can petition for divorce on a number of grounds. The proceedings are often quite lengthy, and it is difficult to establish the grounds for divorce. It can be tied to the other aspects of a woman's potential independence when she does divorce. That's the reality for a lot of women. It's challenging getting child care or paying for it. We were talking about the economy earlier. I think a lot of women stay in marriages not simply because divorce is legally onerous, but because the societal structure for them to financially support themselves and their children is really lacking.

Married women still need their husband's permission to travel. They need it in order to have their passports renewed in certain circumstances. Judges can be very mercurial in applying the law when it comes to divorce cases. There is still very much a culture of, go back and try again, or blaming the woman, or imagining that she should be able to accept her husband's behavior for a variety of regressive reasons. There is a lot of important progress that needs to be brought about in that area.

Can women inherit property?

Yes. And their right to inherit property is protected. It follows the inheritance provisions in Islamic law. I don't think it matches up exactly with what a male child gets, but there are provisions that do ensure that women get their share, even if it's a more limited share.

What about women's health issues?

Iran has a family planning program. It has made great strides in reproductive rights, access to contraception, prenatal and postnatal health care, and abortion. I think the reproduction rate is on the scale of many European societies—two or fewer children per family.

Talk about the contrast between issues facing women in rural areas, which are more conservative, versus the upscale neighborhoods of Tehran and other urban centers.

It's perhaps useful to start with a sense of what that disparity is. Iran is 70 percent urban, 30 percent rural. So a significant percentage of the country remains rural. Over the last forty years there have been great strides in rural Iran in terms of improving roads, irrigation, health care, maternal mortality rates, and more.

But Iran's rural regions do also overlap with its border regions, which overlap with areas where ethnic or religious minorities tend to be congregated. Those communities often have more problems, e.g., child marriage. It still goes on. I hesitate to call them honor killings, but domestic violence, or family-related violence, is still prevalent in a lot of rural areas, despite what I said about material improvements.

Schooling needs far more funding. That's often a grievance that ethnic and religious minorities have. They feel that their regions are neglected. But, that said, many girls' schools in rural areas have computers. They have English-language instruction. It's impressive imagining, or seeing the level of teaching, even in a rural girls' classroom in some far-flung region of Iran.

But I would just underscore that those really entrenched social norms and mores around dating and what's acceptable in public are much more pronounced in rural areas.

The government has targeted gay and transgender people. What's going on? Is the state tapping into some kind of cultural angst?

Well, Iran has a very peculiar history with transgenderism. Khomeini started offering state-sanctioned sex change operations, as a conservative way of dealing with people who are simply homosexual. Under Khomeini, the state started to encourage and even pay for sex change surgery as a way of imposing heterosexual relationships on gay people. That's very controversial in the Islamic world and in the Middle

East. I don't think you would see that anywhere else. It's noteworthy. Although of course, it's quite regressive.

It results in a generation of young men, especially, undergoing these botched surgeries when really they were simply gay, or maybe they were transgender but didn't want to undergo physical surgery. But what does it mean socially? I think Iran is like much of the rest of the region, still a fairly conservative Muslim-majority society in which gay relationships are not socially acceptable to most people. That is a reality. Certainly there are specific areas of the Middle East where there has been a tacit tolerance for men and women being gay, or lesbian, or of a sexual minority background.

In terms of that being legalized, or dealt with on a national level, or in the way that it's been transformed in the West, I just don't think that Muslim-majority societies are there or want to be there. I don't think Iran is distinct in that.

Does gay life have legal protection?

I'm almost certain that every civil code in Muslim-majority countries that's based on Islamic law bans homosexual relations. But is it enforced? Does the state persecute LGBTQI people? Does it go after them? Maybe in Sisi's Egypt, where the state exercises its brutish authority. In Iran, I don't think we've had that kind of thing happen, where it becomes a flashpoint for wider repression.

What's the state's policy regarding prostitution?

The state has attempted to deal with it in various ways. At a certain point, it looked at ways of potentially legalizing prostitution for certain brothels. I think that was under Ahmadinejad. I don't think it went anywhere.

There is also the old custom of temporary marriage. That's always a way where hubs of prostitution, like the shrine and Mashhad for example, could get legal protection for sex workers. They can claim that it's been a temporarily consummated marriage, which is permitted in Shi'a Islam.

This is called segah. *Is it fairly widespread?*

My impression is that it's somewhat reviled among young people. The government has tried all sorts of ways to find an ethical cover to the fact that a whole generation of young people are simply living together outside marriage. They've spoken of "white marriages" and different types of *nikah*, or marriage contracts. But young people don't seem terribly bothered. Perhaps this is generational. Their parents probably disapprove on some level. But it has become so mainstream that the government is trying to contort itself to find ethical patches to cover up what is happening, while young people are just living it.

Are U.S.-imposed sanctions going to generate the outcome that Washington wants, which is regime change in Tehran, or is it going to result in more support for the government?

U.S. pressure and U.S. sanctions have had so many iterations over the last twenty years. This most recent and intense round of it is exceptional in that people very squarely place the blame for Iran's increasing economic hardship on the United States.

It's brought about an awareness and empathy almost for the Iranian position. The government and its mismanagement of the economy and corruption have never looked so blameless in the eyes of Iranians, because it's so patently obvious that in this instance the Islamic republic has the moral high ground. People are increasingly disillusioned and cynical about the West and about the United States, and with that, more sympathetic to the government, while remaining embittered by their disappointments and their grievances with the system.

So the U.S. policy of sanctions and maximum pressure is backfiring. It's shifting Iran away from being a society that was fairly well disposed toward the West. Iran remains out-ward-looking, but it's hard to see how this generation will not be significantly less pro-Western than the last.

In terms of the impact of sanctions, is economic hardship borne more by women than by men?

Definitely. This is something that different researchers, and the organization I work for, the International Crisis Group, are trying to document, to show the specific ways in which women are disproportionately impacted by sanctions. We can see by normative guessing and anecdotally that women tend to become unemployed much more quickly in a sanctions economy. They tend to experience more pressure, because many of them are the ones who handle the family's finances. They handle the food basket and have to do more with less. They bear the brunt of tensions within the family, often. In other countries that have experienced longstanding sanctions, like Venezuela and Cuba, you can map the gender impact of sanctions. I think that we can see this in Iran.

And sanctions impact the prospects for activism. A woman activist who, for example, now has to take on a sec-ond job, or tutoring, or whatever you imagine in order to support her family doesn't have the time anymore for civil society activism. So we can look at it immediately as lowering the horizon and inhibiting that progress, too.

5

THE SLIDE TO WAR
WITH IRAN

Nader Hashemi

May 28, 2019

NADER HASHEMI is the Director of the Center for Middle East Studies at the Josef Korbel School of International Studies at the University of Denver. His articles appear in the *New York Times* and other newspapers and journals. He is the author of *Islam, Secularism and Liberal Democracy* and co-editor of *The People Reloaded*, *The Syria Dilemma*, and *Sectarianization: Mapping the New Politics of the Middle East.*

How have relations between Washington and Tehran evolved since the Iranian Revolution of 1979?

From this moment, relations have always been fraught with deep tension, anxiety, and the potential for conflict. Under Obama, especially after the nuclear agreement was signed in 2015, there was hope that the worst period was behind us. However, it is clear that we are now witnessing the worst moment in U.S.-Iran relations in over forty years. We are at the precipice of a major war in large part due to the policies of Donald Trump.

Is this period more volatile than the hostage crisis?

I think so. While there was a dangerous moment when Jimmy Carter botched a military operation to rescue the hostages in April 1980 that could have led to war, there was never the type of rhetoric that we're hearing today from the president of the United States about regime change, crippling sanctions, and the "obliteration" of Iran. The Trump administration has been instigating the highest level of tension between the two countries since the 1979 revolution.

What is the root cause of Washington's hostility toward Tehran?

Iran has an independent foreign policy. By that, I don't mean it has a necessarily good foreign policy. It has a foreign policy that is independent from direct control and deep dependence on the great powers. This should be contrasted with the period prior to 1979, when Iran was closely allied with the United States and was deeply influenced by Washington. The story begins in 1953 when the United States toppled Prime Minister Mohammad Mossadegh (a liberal-democrat and a secular nationalist) and installed the shah, whose brutal regime remained in power for the next twenty-five years. The nature of the hostility is rooted there. It has little to do with the Islamic Republic's sordid human rights record. Iran has a different vision and pursues policies that clash with the interests of the United States and its allies in the region.

In 2009, there was a presidential election in Iran. Give us the context and the background of what happened.

The sitting president was Mahmoud Ahmadinejad, a bombastic hard-liner. Four years earlier, there was a large-scale boycott of the presidential elections. Many middle-class Iranians did not go to the polls, because they were frustrated with the state of politics, specifically the inability of Iranian reformists, who controlled the presidency and the parliament, to deliver meaningful change. That resulted in Ahmadinejad being elected in 2005. His policies alienated large constituencies within Iran—young people, intellectuals, and women.

In 2009, a moment of opportunity presented itself for the people of Iran. There was an electoral contest between Ahmadinejad, a hawkish conservative backed by the supreme leader and the Islamic Revolutionary Guards Corps (IRGC), versus a moderate reformist candidate who campaigned on a platform of greater democracy, human rights, and better relations with the outside world.

There was a relative opening up of Iran's political society during this moment. For the first time, Iran had presidential debates on television. Millions of Iranians were glued to their TV sets for the back and forth between the candidates. There was massive political mobilization and voter turnout. People stood in lines for a very long time to cast their ballots. The generally accepted figure was that 80 to 85 percent of Iranians voted.

Immediately after the election results were announced in favor of Ahmadinejad, there was a widely held perception that the election had been rigged. A substantial body of evidence has since emerged to substantiate this concern. Ahmadinejad was quickly declared the victor and almost the entire reformist leadership was arrested and forced to undergo a Stalinesque show trial on public television. This led to six months of street protests. State repression was immediate with thousands arrested and tortured, and roughly 150 people were killed. This shocked the ruling clerical establishment and deeply affected the stability of the regime. Mohammad Ali Jafari, the senior commander of the IRGC, said that the protests after the 2009 election were the biggest threat to the survival of the Islamic Republic of Iran since its inception, much greater than the Iran-Iraq War in the 1980s.

The opposition candidate who ran against Ahmadinejad was Mir-Hossein Mousavi. He was prominent in the struggle for democracy, as was his wife, Zahra Rahnavard, a well-known artist, as well as Mehdi Karroubi, a cleric and reformist politician. What has happened to them?

After the 2009 election and the public protests, Khamenei [the supreme leader] ordered an end to public debate on the topic. He validated the results and instructed Iranians to accept them. The opposition leaders refused those instructions. They refused to genuflect before the supreme leader and refused to stay silent about his abuse of political power and growing authoritarianism in Iran. As a result, they were put under house arrest.

The event that actually led to their arrest coincided with the Arab Spring protests in the region in February 2011.

Mousavi and Karroubi called for public demonstrations in solidarity with Tunisia and Egypt. The slogan on the streets of Tehran, which rhymes in Persian, was, "Mubarak, Bin Ali, Now It's Time for Sayyed Ali [Khamenei]." These demonstrations shocked the political establishment and led to the immediate arrest of Mousavi, Rahnavard, and Karroubi. The Islamic Republic of Iran was in a very vulnerable position at that time, because they did not want to be compared to other Arab dictatorships that were facing popular protests calling for democracy.

After these protests broke out in February 2011, there was an incident in the Iranian parliament where hard-line members gathered around the podium of the speaker and publicly called for the execution of Mousavi, Rahnavard, and Karoubi. It looked like a medieval lynch mob event.

Iranian hard-liners were embarrassed and exposed. The regime could not control the narrative. It couldn't stop people from coming into the streets. They were petrified by the comparison being made by the opposition leaders in Iran between the Arab Spring protests for democracy and similar circumstances in the Islamic Republic of Iran. Thus, Mousavi, Rahnavard, and Karroubi were arrested, but never officially charged or put on trial, because doing so would have affected the stability of the Islamic Republic. They remain under house arrest to this day.

How would you characterize the nature of the resistance that culminated around that election?

It was grassroots. It was overwhelmingly middle class and urban-based. Seventy percent of the population live in urban centers now. Having said that, there were people from lower socio-economic classes who participated as well. Most protesters, however, were young people, middle-class men and women. I think the protests were representative of the majority of Iranian society. Of course, the regime's attempt to delegitimize these protests was to make arguments exactly as your question just hinted at—that they were foreign inspired and non-representative of Iranian society.

The regime's official narrative—which is straight out of the "authoritarian playbook"—is that this was an attempt by the CIA and Saudi Arabia to foment changes within Iran that had no indigenous support. This was completely false. The protests lasted consistently for about six months until they were eventually repressed by the regime. That ended what I would call Iran's second moment for democratic transformation.

The first moment being the 1953 period.

No, I was referring to the post-revolutionary period following 1979. Yes, you are correct that during the early

1950s, this was the second moment of democracy during Iran's 20th century (the first being the 1906 Constitutional Revolution). The early 1950s were the best opportunity that Iran had for a democratic transformation. The prospects for democracy at that time looked good. We all know how that story ended, with the CIA-British coup. After the revolution in 1979, I think the first serious moment when there was a lot of optimism for political change and democratization was during the first term of the reformist president,

Mohammad Khatami. This was from roughly 1997 to the year 2000.

Khatami ran on a democratic platform and won. The clerical establishment was completely shocked at his popularity. The first two to three years after the 1997 election brought a revitalization of civil society. Grassroots organizing was widespread. Independent journals and newspapers were flourishing. There were public debates on basic questions like the proper relationship between Islam and democracy, tradition versus modernity, human rights in Iranian society, the legacy of the 1979 Revolution, et cetera.

Parliamentary elections occurred in 2000. Building on the tide of strong support for reform and civil society mobilization, it looked like a new parliament would be elected that would be controlled by reformists. The hope was that with control of two key state institutions—the presidency and the parliament—reformists would advance substantive political change. This did not happen. Iranian hard-liners, seeing control slip from their hands, fought back. Using intimidation, threats, arrests, the court system, and assassinations, the hard-liner-controlled establishment gradually crushed the reformists and rolled back that brief democratic opening. This moment of democracy officially ended in 2005 when Khatami's second term in office concluded. However, in truth, it was effectively over by the summer of 2000.

You write about three moments of democracy in Iran. Could you discuss them?

In the first year and a half after the revolution, there was some political pluralism in Iran. By the time that the Iran-Iraq War began in 1980, effectively, the hard-line Islamists had crushed all dissent and consolidated control. A suffocating political atmosphere took over. National attention was focused on the Iran-Iraq War. Gradually, after the war ended in 1988 and Khomeini died, a period of reconstruction began. Around this time, a series of intellectual debates from within the loyalist camp/supporters of Khomeini also began. These debates are related to the future of Iran and the trajectory of the revolution. Several global trends influenced this debate, such as the end of the Cold War, the expansion of democracy and civil society, and the end of apartheid in South Africa. These forces overlapped with the gradual relaxing of restrictions on civil society and political mobilization related to presidential and parliamentary elections in Iran during the 1990s. During this period, we see the emergence of factional rivalry among supporters of the Islamic Republic that leads to these "moments" of potential democratic transition.

The first one was the 1997 surprise election of Mohammad Khatami, a reformist candidate. He campaigned on a platform of democracy and civil society, and he was a religious intellectual with a keen interest in philosophy and religious reform. There was a widespread sense at the time, especially during his first term, that this might be a transformative moment for Iran.

Long story short, the hard-liner elements of the regime used the courts and various security organizations, primarily the Basij militia [one of the forces of the Islamic Revolutionary Guards Corps], to crush the potential for democracy that was seemingly on the horizon.

This was also when George W. Bush was elected president of the United States and identified Iran as a member of the "Axis of Evil." Some see this as a turning point, because the Bush administration policies significantly undermined the transformations that were taking place in Iran.

My reading is different. This moment of democracy was already crushed by Iranian hard-liners before Bush made his infamous speech. Of course, the policies of the Bush administration after 9/11 indirectly supported the policies of hard-line factions in Iran, a trend that has returned under Trump.

Here we see a long-standing theme of Iranian politics: Hard-liners in the United States call for tough action against Iran, and these policies indirectly bolster their counterparts in Tehran. Hard-liners in Iran play off this rhetoric. In truth, this has a mutually reinforcing effect on both sides of the U.S.-Iran divide.

Thus, 1997 to 2000 was the first moment of post-revolutionary democratic opening. The second one was the Green Movement in 2009. Again, it looked like there was an opportunity for substantive change. According to the regime itself, three million people were on the streets of Tehran in the summer of 2009 calling for political accountability and substantive political reform. That moment, too, was brutally crushed.

It is interesting, if you listen to some of the debates here in the U.S. about the 2009 Green Movement protest, that neo-conservatives and other Republicans blame Obama for not siding with the protesters, for not speaking out strongly in favor of the Green Movement. The reality, I believe, was that Obama played his cards correctly. I'm not a huge fan of Obama, but his response to the Green Movement protest was careful, calculated, and correct in the following sense:

He realized right from the beginning that he didn't want to insert the United States into an internal Iranian political debate over an election and make it easy for Iranian hard-liners to blame street protests on U.S. support.

When the repression increased, Obama did issue statements condemning the repression. The argument that you often hear is that Obama should have spoken out much more vociferously and intervened in the middle of the post-election fury in Iran. I think that would have backfired, and it would have resulted in a greater crackdown on protesters. The Iranian hard-liners would have exploited Obama's statements to paint the protesters as American agents. They would have turned the debate away from a stolen election and internal repression and made it all about the United States.

The third moment of democracy is less clear than the previous two I have mentioned. Sadly, I think it, too, has just passed us by. It began with the 2013 election of President Hassan Rouhani. He campaigned on a platform of greater reforms, increased openness, and freedom for opposition leaders. Critically, the key argument that he advanced was that he wanted to resolve Iran's problem with the international community that pertained to its controversial nuclear program. Rouhani pledged that within a hundred days, he would make progress in that direction—a promise he was successful in achieving. Robust diplomacy led to an interim nuclear agreement in 2013 and a final agreement in 2015.

The political hope that was attached to Rouhani's election was that a nuclear agreement would remove the threat of external military attacks on Iran. This would then allow for sanctions to be lifted. That process, if given enough time, would gradually lead to greater integration, exchange, and openness between Iran and the international community.

Critically, it would allow better economic and social conditions to emerge in Iran. The political benefits that would flow from this new arrangement would be that it would create democratic opportunities for people to organize, mobilize, and to challenge authoritarianism in Iran. This would be in sharp contrast to the period when there was little organizing or opposition as many people were simply fighting for survival, as was the case during the heavy sanction regime imposed by the Obama administration prior to the nuclear agreement. There was a sense among Iranian democratic forces that if given enough time, the economic benefits that would flow from the nuclear agreement would eventually lead to some political openings and changes down the road. I characterize that as Iran's third moment of possible democratic opening, but with a caveat: This moment was not as clear as the two earlier ones were, when the question of democracy, political change, and accountability were much more direct and much more visible for people to see.

During the invasion of Afghanistan following 9/11, Iran was helpful to the United States. In December of 2001 at the Bonn Conference, Iran was instrumental in getting Hamid Karzai selected as president of Afghanistan. Tehran put pressure on its Afghan allies, particularly the Northern Alliance, to make that happen. But in the following month, in his first State of the Union address, George W. Bush labeled Iran an "Axis of Evil" state.

This is correct. After 9/11, the U.S. and Iran had overlapping interests in Afghanistan and Iraq. U.S. policy under Bush 43 was not interested in exploring them, in part because they were drunk on power. Instead, they chose confrontation with Tehran and in the process inadvertently affirmed the ideological narrative of Iranian hard-liners. "You can't trust the United States. You cannot negotiate with them. They will always betray you. If you give them an inch, they will take a mile. We need to rally around the revolutionary flag. We have to constantly be vigilant because the United States is coming to get us."

However, the constituency associated with the Reform Movement—Khatami, Rouhani, Foreign Minister Zarif, and others—have called for political engagement with the

West, including the United States, to resolve tensions via diplomacy. This divide is a major source of tension among Iranian ruling elites.

Talk about how the Islamic Republic's economy is structured and the role of the Islamic Revolutionary Guards Corps as a significant player in the economy.

Iran's economy is comprised of three different sectors: a public sector, a private sector, and a semi-state sector. The semi-state sector consists of a number of religious and revolutionary foundations that have a lot of wealth and their own internal accounting processes that are opaque and not accountable to the public. They employ hundreds of thousands of people, perhaps more. They are involved in significant economic activity.

Part of that semi-state component also includes the IRGC's role in Iran's economy. They own hotels, construction firms, shopping malls, sports teams, et cetera. They are involved in a massive amount of business activity. Iran has a closed political system, so it is difficult to talk with precision in terms of how much of the economic activity is under the direct control of the IRGC. It is widely believed to be roughly 40 percent. This vast sector of the Iranian economy which is in the hands of the IRGC and their affiliated companies includes an extensive network of clients that serve them and whom they employ in exchange for loyalty and benefits. This is one of the reasons why the regime has a base of support. It is minority support, but there are many people whose livelihoods and jobs are dependent on maintaining the political and economic status quo.

Let us look at one example. In a famous case in 2004, a contract was given to a Turkish cellular phone company to build a mobile phone network in Iran. The deal was signed and sealed. The IRGC protested. Eventually, the deal was broken. The contract was then given to the IRGC to develop a cellular phone system. This is a reflection of the type of the influence that they wield.

It is very difficult to rein them in, because they are so deeply integrated into the DNA of the Islamic Republic. To his credit, Rouhani has tried to diminish their economic influence, but this effort was dropped after Trump implemented his plan to strangle Iran's economy and possibly bring about regime change.

The IRGC is a big reason why Iran's economy did not function up to the level that many people expected after the nuclear deal. The standard narrative is that the reason why Iran's economy is in shambles is because of U.S. sanctions. While this is true, this narrative clouds the full picture. The other aspect is internal corruption, mismanagement, and the absence of an open business climate where there are clear rules and transparency, where private businesses can bid on contracts, and where there can be some fair regulation of business activity that is adjudicated by an independent court system. All of this is missing, and it contributes to Iran's current economic crisis.

Do you see any similarities between this situation with the IRGC in Iran and the military in Pakistan and Egypt?

There are lots of similarities and parallels. Differences emerge when we talk about the specifics. In many ways, in the case of Pakistan, and many other developing societies, the military is the most powerful institution. It is responsible for external security and internal repression if things get out of control. They often have a huge stake in the economic activity of the country in ways that I have just described. Egypt fits this pattern, too. It is estimated that up to 40 percent of the Egyptian economy is controlled, directly or indirectly, by the military and its offshoots.

In April 2019 the IRGC was declared to be a foreign terrorist organization by the Trump administration. What has been the impact?

Mostly it has had a political and psychological impact. First, it makes no sense to declare the IRGC a terrorist organization. Not because they don't deserve the label. They are involved in many nasty things internally and regionally, especially in Syria. Remember, Iran was already under heavy sanctions prior to this declaration. Many senior members of the regime, including senior IRGC leaders, were already singled out for sanctions.

The designation of the IRGC as a terrorist organization is primarily for domestic consumption in the United States. It was also an attempt by the Trump administration to send a message to Iran that we are coming after you. It took place against the backdrop of crippling sanctions, and attempts to apply sanctions not just on Iran's oil and gas sector, but sanctions on its steel, mining, shipping, and transportation industries.

This IRGC terror designation was also being pushed by Iran hawks in the U.S. who were hoping to close the doors to diplomacy. Labeling anyone who has any connection to the IRGC as a terrorist blocks any meeting with anyone who has an IRGC affiliation. It effectively limits what can be done in terms of diplomacy and dialogue. Remember, Iran's Supreme Leader Khamenei is the commander in chief of the IRGC. Thus, any dialogue with him or his representatives now becomes much more difficult.

Washington's proclamation says, "We will continue to increase financial pressure and raise the costs on the Iranian regime for its support of terrorist activity until it abandons its malign and outlaw behavior." The terms "malign actor" and "bad actor" come up frequently in discussions about Iran. Even in the polite discourse of NPR's flagship news programs, Morning Edition *and* All Things Considered, *and the* PBS NewsHour, *it's a given that Iran is engaging in malign behavior.*

Agreed. My response is, yes, Iran is involved in and has contributed to destabilizing the Middle East—but it is not the only bad actor that has contributed to regional instability.

I think Iran is most guilty in terms of what it has done in Syria over the last eight years. From day one, it has been backing a morally reprehensible regime and has been involved in and complicit with massive war crimes and crimes against humanity.

Iran is also guilty of furthering sectarianism in Iraq. I think in other theaters of conflict, in Yemen, Iran's role is grossly exaggerated in the Western discourse on the topic. In Lebanon, it has played a significant and polarizing role by supporting Lebanese Shi'a forces: Hezbollah.

We need to take a step back to objectively understand the roots of instability in the Middle East. When we do, the one-sided Washington narrative does not stand up to scrutiny. The dominant view from Washington, which has sunk deep roots in American political culture, is that the main reason why the Middle East is unstable today is because of Iran's malign activity. Period. Full stop. This is distortion of reality.

The fact is, there are other bad actors who have contributed to Middle East turmoil. Saudi Arabia and the spread of Wahhabi Islam is a huge part of the problem. The United Arab Emirates is a big part of the problem, as are the policies of Israel both in the past and especially under Benjamin Netanyahu. The ongoing, systematic oppression, suppression, and dispossession of the Palestinian people has been a source for regional destabilization for over seventy years.

To focus all of our attention on Iran completely distorts the objective reality of why this region is in turmoil. It also ignores the underlying socio-economic and political roots of the discontent that is destabilizing the region.

The Guardian *published a map of U.S. bases in Afghanistan, Kuwait, Turkey, Iraq, the UAE, Djibouti, Qatar, Bahrain, Saudi Arabia, and Jordan. They literally surround Iran.*

Iran is surrounded by the United States with military bases and naval forces that almost encircle it. The perception in the U.S.

is the opposite—Iran is the main aggressor and is threatening American national security. As a result, we have to go war.

In the American foreign policy discourse, there is an inbuilt assumption that the United States and its allies are judged by a different standard and allowed to do whatever they wants in terms of their projection of power. This is called the "home team" advantage. It is understandable when the government officials work within this framework; serious journalists should work outside of it.

Secretary of State Mike Pompeo, a former CIA director, and John Bolton, former Trump national security advisor, have had a particular animus toward Iran.

I would actually take it a step further. It is more than an animus. It is actually an obsession. It's an obsession that almost defies rational explanation. Their level of hawkishness is less about the individuals themselves and more about the political forces that back their careers.

On one level, the individuals themselves are part of the story. Pompeo is known to be a Christian fundamentalist. On an evangelical television station, he actually said that it is within the realm of possibility that God has sent Donald Trump to save Israel from Iran. At the same time, he does have deep ties to U.S. weapons manufacturers, Boeing in particular. Pompeo is part of the constituency that strongly supports ongoing arms sales to Saudi Arabia and the United Arab Emirates, and backs Israel unconditionally.

In the case of John Bolton, there is his own individual personal hawkishness. But he too has ties to nefarious forces both in Washington and in the region that are pushing for a military confrontation with Iran.

How did Bolton become the National Security Advisor? Read Dexter Filkins's article in *The New Yorker*. He comes pretty close to saying that the reason why H.R. McMaster was replaced by Bolton was because of the lobbying efforts of Sheldon Adelson, the hawkish multibillionaire whose fanatical views on Israel/Palestine include the belief that Palestinians do not have human rights. He convinced Trump to appoint Bolton as his National Security Advisor in return for political support.

In addition, the very powerful and influential constituency of right-wing hawkish supporters of Benjamin Netanyahu in the U.S., whose politics on the Middle East overlap with Bolton's worldview, are part of this story, as are Saudi Arabia and the United Arab Emirates. This core constituency desperately wants the U.S. to launch a war against Iran. These actors have had their own lobbyists in Washington and have been working overtime. They also have the ear of the White House.

For this reason, the prospects of a war will remain high between now and the next presidential election. War hawks see this as an excellent opportunity, with Trump in the White House, that might not exist after November 2020.

Pompeo also has said that the Bible "informs everything I do." If someone from the Taliban said something like that, they'd be deemed just another religious crazy.

David Friedman, the U.S. Ambassador to Israel, made a similar statement. He claimed that God is on the side of Israel and Netanyahu. With respect to the broader Middle East, and Iran in particular, these actors have fanatical views. The influence of evangelicals and Likudniks are some of the most dangerous elements that influence the Trump administration's Middle East policy.

Talk about the painstakingly negotiated Iran Deal. It was a breakthrough moment in U.S.-Iran relations and Iran's relations with the other permanent members of the U.N. Security Council and Germany, plus the European Union.

This is a very important story that represents a high point in terms of better relations between Iran and the United States. Trita Parsi's book *Losing an Enemy* covers this topic very well, as does Robin Wright's coverage in *The New Yorker*.

In short, due to the convergence of forward-looking leaders in Washington and Tehran, both governments seriously pursued diplomacy. An agreement was reached in 2015 that required Iran to roll back its nuclear program and placed it under international inspection, in exchange for sanctions relief. This agreement was supported by nearly the entire world and culminated in U.N. Security Council resolution 2231 (2015). It was a major step forward in terms of enhancing international peace and security.

Trump tore up the agreement in 2018 and pursued a policy of "maximum pressure" against Iran. His real problem with the nuclear agreement was not its content but the fact it was negotiated by Obama. I am certain Trump never read the actual document.

What happens with neighboring Turkey, which has been heavily dependent on Iranian oil?

Turkey stopped purchasing Iranian oil in May 2019 because of the pressure that the U.S. placed on all countries that trade with Iran. There were waivers that were given to countries that were purchasing Iranian oil, giving them a period of several months to find other sources of oil or be subject to new U.S. sanctions. The one exception has been that China still buys Iranian oil. This, of course, over-laps with the trade crisis that exists between China and the United States today, giving Beijing some leverage in chal-lenging the U.S. position.

The bottom line here is that Iran's ability to export its oil shrank significantly in 2018 and 2019. The Iranian economy is in free fall. Inflation is officially at 37 percent, according to government statistics (which means that in reality it is far worse). Unemployment has skyrocketed. The International Monetary Fund predicted that Iran's economy would con-tract by 6 percent in 2019. The value of the Iranian cur-rency has been cut in half. You have a situation in Iran today where, literally, people are struggling to survive, trying to figure out how to make ends meet. There is no mass starva-tion, but poverty levels have skyrocketed.

And if you're wondering about your next meal, how you're going to get medicine for your ailing parents, you can't be thinking about social change too much.

American sanctions have had a catastrophic effect on the struggle for democracy in Iran. This is why the indigenous grassroots leaders and civil society organizations within Iran have strongly supported the nuclear deal and were extremely critical of Trump's hard-line policy of crippling sanctions. At a demonstration at one of the most prestigious universities in Tehran, Allameh Tabataba'i University, the slogans were very revealing: "No to war. No to sanctions. No to authoritarianism. Freedom for political prisoners. The policy of sanctions is inhuman. National security is meaningless without freedom and democracy."

In these slogans, you see two main targets: U.S. sanctions policy and the internal repression by the regime. These two themes are deeply linked now, because you cannot have a struggle for democracy when the economy has collapsed and people are struggling to figure out where their next meal is going to come from.

Sanctions are a form of collective punishment.

Yes. The official U.S. claim is that sanctions on the Islamic Republic of Iran are aimed at changing the regime's behavior. The senior leaders are the targets. But the sanctions do not directly affect these elite elements of Iranian society. We know this from other cases, including Iraq in the 1990s, when strong punitive sanctions devastated Iraqi society, but strengthened Saddam Hussein.

The same applies to Iran. The IRGC has its smuggling networks, its bank accounts, and its alternative forms of

income. The average citizen who does not have those ties
are the ones really being hit hard by these sanctions.

*On my last trip to Iran a couple of years ago, I met two
students who had applied to U.S. universities and have sub-
sequently been denied visas because of the travel ban. They
were so disappointed. You must know of similar cases.*

I have an Iranian student at the University of Denver who
was accepted into our master's program. He couldn't begin
in September because of Trump's anti-Muslim travel ban.
He finally arrived four months later, right at the time when
sanctions were starting to have a deep effect. He couldn't pay
his tuition. His parents couldn't afford it due to the drop in
the value of Iranian currency. He is struggling to make ends
meet and now is looking to transfer to another school that
costs less. Therefore, yes, many Iranians admire U.S. society,
the education system, and the freedoms that exist. They don't
admire U.S. foreign policy, because it is adversely hurting
Iranians for policies over which they have little control.

I can tell you many other stories as to how the policies that the United States has pursued have inadvertently
hurt the average Iranian while strengthening the regime.
Something as simple as opening a bank account is extremely
difficult if you happen to be Iranian living in the U.S. or

Europe. If the bank finds out there is any transfer of money to or from Iran, to pay things like tuition, the bank account is shut down. If you are Iranian, it is almost impossible to travel to the United States today.

This is one of the huge ironies that exposes the Trump/Pompeo claim that they "support the Iranian people." If they really want to support the Iranian people, then why is there a travel ban on Iranians that prevents them from coming to the United States? Remember, most of these people are not responsible for the policies of the regime; in most cases, they are critical of the Islamic Republic. It doesn't matter. Trump/Pompeo prefer a policy of collective punishment as this allows them to look tough and is strongly supported by their core constituency.

What about medical supplies?

Medical supplies are also affected by sanctions. Not officially, but when financial transactions with Iran are sanctioned and the value of the currency drops, this makes access to medicines more difficult. The result is a serious increase in basic health problems that normally can be treated. Physicians' organizations and hospitals in Iran frequently complain about the inability to access basic medicines. It results in a lot of unneeded suffering that is directly related to U.S. sanctions.

How would you rate the New York Times *coverage of Iran?*

There has been this depiction of Iran's behavior that often exaggerates the threat and contributes to pro-war hysteria. But there has also been some very thoughtful and sound reporting as well. The *New York Times* had a very good reporter in Tehran, Thomas Erdbrink. Farnaz Fassihi has taken over and has done an excellent job. Its editorial page has gotten a lot better. On the negative side, there have been hawkish and incendiary headlines that have fed the war narrative. There is a lot of room for criticism, but among the major U.S. newspapers, it is far from the worst, and it has been much better than in the past.

What about the U.S. attack on Iraq and the hysteria in 2002 and 2003 about mushroom clouds, mobile chemical labs, and weapons of mass destruction?

It seems like déjà vu all over again, doesn't it? In the lead-up to the 2003 war, Iraq was portrayed as a threat not only to the United States but a threat to the entire world.

Given the disastrous outcome of this war, today we see much more opposition to this fearmongering in Congress, and also in the broader society. David Frum, an influential Republican intellectual, recently wrote an essay in *The Atlantic* saying, "I made a mistake in 2003. I contributed to that war. Let's not make the same mistake today with Iran." You know things have changed when you read this from pen of Mr. Frum.

It is an important intellectual development. People close to the Bush administration, who were directly involved in the 2003 Iraq War narrative, are now issuing mea culpas and saying, "Look, let's not make that mistake again." This suggests that some lessons have been learned and U.S. political culture is not in favor of another war in the Middle East. Given this reality, there is some room for cautious optimism.

On the other side of the ledger, we have Israel, Saudi Arabia, and the Emirates gunning for war. They all have access to the president's ear. Ironically enough, Trump himself may be the chief figure preventing a military conflict with Iran. He has issued contradictory statements, but a consistent line we hear is that he wants to have a dialogue with Iran in contrast to his hawkish advisors and Middle East allies. He is not in favor of war. While his Iran strategy is very unclear, my best guess is that Trump is seeking an ego boost. He seems to be aiming for another North Korea–style summit where he gets lots of recognition and praise for doing something that Obama could not do: get a public meeting with Rouhani.

Trump says repeatedly that he simply doesn't want Iran to have a nuclear weapon, but has he actually read the 2015 nuclear agreement with Iran? It accomplishes precisely this goal. We do have this internal policy debate in the White House between Iran hawks and Trump, who hasn't signed on to an all-out military strike against Iran . . . yet.

As we move forward, I suspect the aim among the war hawks may very well be to try to convince the president that a strike on Iran could be a good thing for his reelection.

The International Atomic Energy Agency (IAEA), the U.N. organization that monitored Iranian sites, said that the country was in full compliance with the conditions of the Iran Deal.

The same can be said about several senior members of Trump's own cabinet. James Mattis and H.R. McMaster confirmed that Iran was living up to the terms of the agreement. Some issues are controversial in Middle East politics and in U.S.-Iran relations. This is one where there is zero controversy. Iran lived up to its obligations under the nuclear agreement. It is a simple fact that even extreme war hawks acknowledge.

What did you make of the president's boast that it will be "the end" of Iran if there is a war with the United States?

It is obviously a point of deep concern. It highlights Trump's volatility and his unpredictability. A few days earlier, he was calling for negotiations with Iran.

"They should call me," he said.

In fact, the president of Switzerland, Ueli Maurer, was in Washington at the time. Trump passed on a telephone number to the Swiss to give to Iran. Switzerland represents U.S. interests in Iran. Trump then went on to make the statement about annihilating Iran. The next day, he was talking about negotiations again.

What is my own reading of President Trump's view on Iran? He clearly hasn't read the Iran nuclear agreement. If he had, he wouldn't be making these ridiculous claims that this is the "worst deal ever negotiated" in human history. In addition, a big part of Trump's opposition to the Iran nuclear deal is simply the fact that it has Barack Obama's name on it.

My concern is that Trump will be easily manipulated by much more sinister and savvy individuals within his inner orbit and his close allies in the region. Given the erratic nature of this president, many of his statements are incoherent and contradictory. It does not leave one with a sense of confidence that somehow, diplomacy will prevail, and war might be avoided.

What would it take to establish diplomatic relations with Iran?

It would require a new American president who is committed to diplomacy and a fundamental transformation of the structure of power within Iran. I believe the biggest obstacle to diplomatic relations lies in Tehran, not in Washington. There is strong opposition in Iran (among hard-liners, not at the popular level) to diplomatic negotiations and relations with the U.S. for reasons that have to do with internal Iranian politics and the regime's crisis of internal legitimacy. This requires an external enemy to sustain the Islamic Republic's core identity. The basic identity that gives shape and unites hard-line factions as a political group is rooted in a deep and unrelenting ideological opposition to the United States. Under Supreme Leader Khamenei, I cannot see diplomatic relations taking place. Khamenei is eighty years old. He is going to die sometime in the next decade. Possibly, there will be an opportunity down the road, but not given the existing structure of power inside Iran today.

What do you make of this notion of a Shi'a arc?

The Shi'a arc is a term that was coined by King Abdullah of Jordan in 2004. It was a statement made to argue that Iran was taking over the Middle East. It was a reflection of the changing regional dynamics that took place primarily in Iraq after the U.S. invasion in 2003—which included, ironically, the rise of Shi'a political parties in Iraq that had close connections with Iran. Pro-U.S. authoritarian regimes in the Arab world feared that the balance of power could shift in Iran's direction. In short, what these repressive regimes really feared was political change, a free press, political pluralism, free and fair elections. King Abdullah of Jordan, the House of Saud in Saudi Arabia, the dictators in the United Arab Emirates do not really fear Shi'a Islam or Iran. This is just an excuse. Their real fear is any form of opposition—religious or secular—that might challenge authoritarian rule in the Arab world. This is monumental and animates their thinking and shapes their policies and rhetoric.

Arab autocracies display a similar form of paranoia and fear against the Muslim Brotherhood today. Given that the Muslim Brothers are Sunni, you cannot play the sectarian card if you are an Arab dictator. Instead, you play the terrorist card and hope to get a sympathetic hearing in the West.

Despotic regimes try hard to convince the United States that the Muslim Brotherhood should be labeled a terrorist organization. But their real fear is losing political power. These regimes don't believe in sharing power or relinquishing it. They are political tyrannies of varying degrees. Their obsession with Iran starts in 1979 after the Iranian Revolution. This seismic event demonstrated an alternative example of how Muslims can be political, and in the process of doing so, bring about political change by confronting authoritarian regimes. These countries have been rightly described as the "Axis of Arab Autocracies." Their ruling elites naively believe that if somehow Iran can be contained or crushed, their political problems will disappear, along with political Islam. If you just think about it for a moment, the revolts and protests that broke out during the Arab Spring had nothing to do with Iran. The claims of these Arab despotic regimes are entirely bogus, but like all authoritarian leaders, they seek to blame their problems on external actors, never themselves.

The 2011 Arab Spring uprisings were fundamentally about opposing political tyranny, the lack of social justice, and the expansion of authoritarianism. People revolted because they wanted a better future. In fact, the model that people were pointing to was not the Islamic Republic of Iran. It was Erdogan in Turkey when he was observing democratic norms. This is prior to the 2013 Gezi Park protests, when politics in Turkey were more democratic and inclusive. Many Arabs were pointing to this model and saying we want to emulate this where we live.

This notion of a Shi'a crescent is one of the many obsessions that these authoritarian regimes have. It is effectively a strategy to deflect demands for political change. It tries to play the sectarian card—seeking to mobilize people around sectarian identities in order to shift the conversation away from dictatorship, demands for democracy, demands for political accountability and human rights. It tries to mobilize Sunnis around the narrative that Shi'a Islam is taking over.

Iran is what Edward Said would call the Other—non-Arabic-speaking, different ethnically, culturally. Its civilization had developed along different lines from its Arab neighbors.

Arab dictators seek to exploit this perceived sense of otherness, to mobilize people around the sectarian/ethno-nationalist narrative. They are not part of us; they represent a theological heresy; Arab Shi'a are loyal to Iran, not to their nation-state, et cetera. In the official rhetoric that comes out of Saudi Arabia, there are constant reference to Iranians as fire worshippers. They are Zoroastrians. They are not really Muslims. They are an evil force that must be confronted. Sometimes, you will hear the term Safavi thrown into the equation, which is related to the 16th-century dynasty that ruled Iran.

That made Shi'a Islam the national religion.

Correct. Before 1501, Iranians were overwhelmingly Sunnis.

In closed authoritarian societies today, when you control the narrative, at least the official narrative on state television, it is easy to mobilize people. But let us also be clear, Iranian foreign policy has made it easier for Arab despots to deploy this narrative.

Iran has played a role in Syria that has been very destructive, and its role in Iraq has contributed to sectarianism. Of course, Arab dictatorships have deliberately amplified this narrative and have used Iran's regional aggression as a way to fundamentally shift attention away from their own corrupt and incompetent rule and to try to place all of the region's problems at Iran's doorstep.

What gives you hope?

What gives me hope is not the short term. The picture looks very bleak.

Within Iran, if you talk to young Iranians, if you engage with them, if you travel around the country, you will see an educated, globally connected society that yearns for political change and has moderate views about the world. Yes, there is a deep strain of chauvinistic nationalism that exists, but it doesn't dominate political attitudes. This exists everywhere, including in the United States.

Most Iranians want to engage with the international community. They want to travel to the United States. They want their government in Tehran to be more democratic, liberal, secular, and accountable. We often ignore these important societal forces that have emerged within Iran, because the conversation in the United States is all about Iran's regional behavior, tensions with the United States, threats against Israel, et cetera.

Fact: The battle for ideas is *over* in Iran. Those ideas have been overwhelmingly won by reformist forces, by democratic forces who believe in certain fundamental basic principles: democracy, universal human rights, the separation of religion and state. These are values that many Iranians aspire to achieve. Of course, they can't articulate them and translate those desires into institutional and political change, because they are living in a deeply authoritarian regime. But they are trying, and sadly, U.S. policy is not on their side.

The political values among young people, both in terms of what they want from their own society, and Iran's relationship with the outside world, overlap with what I think many Americans want in terms of their relationship with Iran—views more rooted in diplomacy, in peace, in international law, in fruitful exchanges between societies, mutual learning, and respect. These are my long-term hopes.

PART TWO

January 1, 2020

How would you characterize the demonstrations that began on November 15, 2019, in response to a sharp increase in gasoline prices? Compare the protests today with those of 2009 and late 2017 to 2018. You told Qantara.de *that the 2009 protests "were overwhelmingly nonviolent." And talk about what you call the "changing class composition" of those turning out in the streets.*

The biggest differences between these protests were in the following areas: economic class, geography, and ideology. In 2009, the protests were mostly middle class, they took place in major cities, and were connected ideologically to the process of political reform and in support of reformist politicians Mir-Hossein Mousavi and Mehdi Karroubi, who participated in the presidential election in June 2009. By contrast, the protests in 2017–2018 and in November 2019 drew participation from mostly lower economic classes, comprised of young unemployed men in small cities and towns and the poorer sections of major cities, without any known leadership or political affiliation.

The final difference is the form the protests took. In 2009, they were overwhelmingly nonviolent, while the 2017–2018 and 2019 protests involved attacks on banks, government buildings, and petrol stations. It should be clearly stated, however, that in 2019 most of the violence was on the side of security forces. Many peaceful protesters were also attacked by police and plainclothes officials connected to the IRGC. Credible evidence exists of the deliberate destruction of property by the security forces to tarnish the reputation of protesters. This makes sense to me. When it comes to regime survival, the Islamic Republic observes very few moral limits.

In terms of numbers, the mayor of Tehran stated that in one of the major protests on June 15, 2009, three million people were in the streets. During the November 2019 protests, Yadollah Javani, a senior IRGC leader, stated that twenty-nine out of the thirty-one provinces in Iran experienced demonstrations. The minister of interior in 2019 put the number of people involved in the nationwide demonstrations at 200,000. I suspect the number was much higher.

The changing class composition and the more radical slogans of the protesters make sense to me. Over the past decade, the level of poverty and inequality has increased in

Iran; so has the level of citizen frustration and anger. The political system has grown more authoritarian, and the credibility of reformist politicians has been tarnished due to their inability to bring about significant change.

One final observation about the November 2019 protests. Some of the biggest protests—and subsequent deaths—took place in the south and west of Iran, in areas inhabited by ethnic and religious minorities. This also makes sense, given the widespread ethnic and religious discrimination that exists among these sectors of society. They also experience higher levels of unemployment, and for all of these reasons there is deep-seated discontent.

You cite a statement from the Iranian Writers Association. What did they say? And what has civil society in general been saying about the protests and the state response to them?

In a piece I wrote for the *New York Times* (December 18, 2019), I noted that "historians will record the blood-soaked days of November" (2019) as "the worst mass killing of protesters in modern Iranian history." These events deeply shocked and scarred society. A reflection of this mood can be found in the various statements put out from civil society groups (writers, physicians, unions, students). The Iranian Writers Association statement read:

*Every corner of Iran is mourning the atrocities left
behind from the confrontation between the people
and the authorities. The monster, who previously
silenced the people with deceitful fangs of intimidation and oppression and interrogated free thinkers
and activists in dark dungeons, held them for long
periods, tried them behind closed doors, imprisoned
them based on forced confessions, and banned them
for working or leaving the country, has now put its
secret detention centers at the disposal of unknown
agencies and openly assaulted protesters with bullets
for shouting what they had held back in their throat.*

*Fearing that the truth would reach the world, Iran
became the first state to resort to the darkest form
of censorship by cutting all access to the internet
and imposing complete silence in order to fire bullets at protesters who, like their forefathers in the
1905 Constitutional Revolution, have been fighting
for a better life, while being denied the most basic
human rights, happiness, a future, beauty, art and
culture, and even the right to make a living.*

*By cutting off the internet nationwide, the authori-
ties not only silenced the people of Iran but also*

wasted resources and brought great harm to their livelihood. A huge portion of the country's economic wealth was spent on unprecedented efforts to prevent the people from connecting with the world through cyberspace, while the regime's forces used false excuses to justify suppressing protesters' chants by violently arresting and killing thousands.

Why has the state response been so violent?

Since the 2009 Green Movement protests, and especially since 2015, after the signing of the Iranian nuclear agreement, Iranian hard-liners have felt power slipping from their hands. In response, they have stepped up the repression of society. During the November 2019 protests, the security forces of the Islamic Republic launched what Amnesty International described as a "killing spree." We do not know the precise number killed, but five hundred people seems to be an accurate estimate, based on reporting from credible sources. Some reports suggest the actual number is over a thousand. To date, the regime has not released official figures.

From its inception, the Islamic Republic has adopted a model of neo-Stalinist repression to deal with dissent. This has included censorship, imprisonment of dissidents, assassinations, forced TV confessions derived from torture, and massive amounts of state propaganda. During the November 2019 protests, for example, the family of a slain protester told the Center for Human Rights in Iran that they were warned by the regime if they "spoke to the media, they would dig up his body and take it away." While state-sanctioned repression has ebbed and flowed over the decades, it has gotten decidedly worse in recent years and shows no signs of abating. At its core, the Islamic Republic of Iran remains a police state.

Part of the upsurge in the use of state-sanctioned violence can be explained by international and regional developments. Trump's policy of "maximum pressure" and crippling sanctions aims to bring Iran to its knees. If possible, "regime change" is the optimal outcome, as explicitly stated by senior members of Trump's foreign policy team. This has added to the regime's anxiety and paranoia and led to increased internal repression.

Mass protests in Lebanon and Iraq in late 2019 have added to these anxieties among Iranian leaders. These protests challenge the heavy investment Iran has made in both countries. In Iraq, there are explicit calls for the removal of Iranian influence. In Lebanon, the restructuring of the political system, as protesters are demanding, will be disadvantageous to Iran's key regional ally, Hezbollah, which is currently benefiting from the political status quo.

It is important to point out that many of these protesters—especially in Iraq—are Shi'a Muslims who previously were sympathetic to Iranian foreign policy but are now demanding substantive political and economic reform and the removal of external influences in their country. These regional dynamics have heightened fears in Tehran and can partially explain why the regime has reacted so brutally during the November 2019 protests. Domestically, regionally, and internationally the Islamic Republic is facing challenges that have no parallel during the four decades since the 1979 Revolution.

Do the protests constitute a major threat to the Islamic Republic of Iran?

The Islamic Republic perceives them as a major threat, but I do not see the regime collapsing any time soon. First, the Islamic Republic does have an internal base of support. This is composed of people who are ideologically devoted to clerical rule plus those who are not ideologues but who benefit economically from the political status quo and the vast patronage system that employs millions of people. This segment of society (about 20 percent) will participate in street protests and vote for regime candidates during parliamentary and presidential elections (which are never free, due to the screening of candidates by the Guardian Council).

More broadly, the regime controls the means of production, access to information (shutting down of the internet), and the means of violence. On the other side, the opposition to the Islamic Republic is fragmented; it lacks a courageous leadership, economic resources, or a clear strategy to bring about political change.

How do you navigate between supporting human rights and democratic forces in Iran without playing into Washington's imperial framework?

This is an excellent question. One of the worst things to do is allow U.S. foreign policy to determine your moral compass. For many of our friends on the left, political positions and ethical frameworks are determined by what U.S. policy happens to be toward a particular conflict—and then reversing it 180 degrees. For example, in this warped moral framework, if Washington is opposed to Bashar al-Assad, then Assad should be viewed sympathetically (or in some extreme cases supported, because he is part of an alleged "axis of resistance").

How to navigate the way forward? One of the important ideas I have learned from Noam Chomsky regarding human rights advocacy, is the importance of being a good listener and being modest. This ethical framework is rooted in the idea that before prescribing solutions to problems that affect other people, one should first exercise a degree of humility. Do not assume a priori that you know the answers or have the best strategy. If you are serious about human rights and pro-democracy activism, it is morally imperative to seek out the views of those you are seeking to help and who are most directly affected by human rights abuses; to listen to those voices who have organic connections to their own societies, and who are on the front line of the struggle. Their advice should inform your perspective and activism. In other words, before adopting a political strategy and supporting a specific policy, ask pro-democracy activists and human rights campaigners within country X: "How can we in the West/USA best help your struggle?"

In the context of Iran, the following recommendations reflect a broad consensus among Iranian human rights activists and pro-democracy intellectuals whom I have interviewed and studied. Those who are genuinely interested in understanding the internal Iranian debate on human rights and democracy are advised to respect these guidelines and red lines.

Keep the global spotlight on Iran's human rights record; name and sanction individuals directly involved in human rights abuses.

Oppose foreign-based "regime change" policies, especially military adventurism by the United States and its regional allies (i.e., a strong repudiation of Trump/Pompeo/Netanyahu/MBS policy toward Iran).

Oppose broad-based economic sanctions that affect average Iranian citizens and are a form of collective punishment. Targeted sanctions against human rights abusers and high regime officials with blood on their hands are welcomed, even if this cannot be publicly affirmed within Iran among human rights activists.

Support the Iranian nuclear agreement—JCPOA—because it reduces the prospects for war, removes economic sanctions, and opens Iran up to the international community (i.e., yes, to diplomacy).

Support nonviolent strategies for political change as the best way forward. This suggests patience and a long-term approach to advancing human rights and democracy. There are no quick fixes. Stated differently, the struggle for democracy and human rights in Iran is a marathon, not a sprint.

Give recognition to and elevate the work of human rights and pro-democracy defenders within Iran, especially those who are incarcerated. Key figures include Nasrin Sotoudeh, Nargess Mohammadi, Ismail Bakhshi, Sepideh Gholian, and many others.

Michael Safi, writing in The Guardian, *says, "Unless the U.S. reverses course on its 'maximum pressure' strategy against Iran, 2020 is likely to be another year of misery for ordinary Iranians and danger in the Middle East."*

Michael Safi is a good journalist covering the Middle East, and he is absolutely correct.

In October 2019, Human Rights Watch released a report called "Maximum Pressure: U.S. Economic Sanctions Harm Iranians' Right to Health." This report noted that these sanctions "pose a serious threat to Iranians' right to health and access to essential medicines." Some of the "worst-affected are Iranians with rare diseases and/or conditions that require specialized treatment who are unable to acquire previously available medicines or supplies. This includes people with leukemia, epidermolysis bullosa (EB, a type of disease that causes fragile, blistering skin), or epilepsy, and individuals with chronic eye injuries from exposure to chemical weapons during the Iran-Iraq war."

U.S. sanctions—which are opposed by almost the entire world—have severely crippled the Iranian economy. Inflation has gone from 9 percent before the sanctions to roughly 40 percent today. Unemployment has skyrocketed, as many businesses have been forced to close or lay off employees. Iran's economy grew by over 10 percent in 2016; after the sanctions were implemented it contracted by 6 percent.

U.S. officials often brag about these results. They link them to a plan for regime change, hoping that these sanctions will provoke a revolution. Mike Pompeo has given interviews that explicitly make this connection, and in the process, he has confirmed the worldview of Iranian hard-liners.

It is important to note that it is the average Iranian citizen, not members of the ruling elite or the Revolutionary Guards, who are most hurt by these sanctions.

Cyber and economic warfare are part of Washington's Iran strategy. In mid-2019 you feared the possibility of a U.S. military attack. Do you still feel that way?

There were two moments in 2019 when the possibility of a major U.S.-Iran war seemed imminent. The first event was in late June, when, after a mutual shooting down of each other's drones in the Persian Gulf, Trump gave the order to launch a military strike on Iran. According to him, the U.S. military was "locked and loaded" for a strike. At the last moment, he changed his mind.

The other event was in mid-September, when Iran launched a surprise attack on Saudi oil facilities. This took 50 percent of Saudi oil off the market and led to heighten tensions. Many thought that Trump would respond militarily, but he did not (to the horror of his regional allies).

How to explain the absence of U.S. military response against Iran in both of these cases? There have been two schools of thought among Trump's foreign policy team with respect to Iran: the extreme war hawks led by Mike Pompeo, Rudolph Giuliani, Jared Kushner, and the now departed John Bolton, and the isolationist voices led by Senator Rand Paul, Tucker Carlson, and Steve Bannon. Both groups support harsh sanctions on Iran, but the latter group opposes military action against Iran, because it could drag the U.S. into another war in the Middle East. Trump has sided with the latter group.

He has also made a series of statements that indicate he wants to strike a new nuclear deal with Iran. To the shock of his many pro-Israel and pro-Saudi supporters, he has even said that if Iran agrees to negotiate with him, they could become "a wealthy country," Trump could be Iran's "best friend," and that he aspired to "make Iran great again."

My own view is that I seriously doubt Trump can locate Iran on the map. He aspires to forge a new deal with Iran that has his name on it, not Obama's. If he manages to accomplish this, he can then claim a major foreign policy success, while basking in the glow of a summit meeting with Iran's President Hassan Rouhani (along the lines of the free publicity he got from meeting with Kim Jong Un).

What are the chances of a secular democratic government in Iran? Has the post–November 2019 uprising increased those chances?

I am optimistic about the prospects for a democratic transition in Iran, not in the short term but in the medium term. U.S. foreign policy is a critical factor that influences the prospects for democracy in Iran. Allow me to explain.

The preconditions for democracy in Iran look promising. The standard theoretical requirements that social scientists have identified are all in place. There is a sizable middle class, a political culture that supports democratic norms (among key segments of society and the opposition), and high levels of literacy (including among women). Moreover, after forty years of authoritarianism, the Islamic Republic faces a deep and expanding crisis of legitimacy that senior Iranian leaders have openly admitted. Young people, who constitute the bulk of the population, are overwhelmingly political and socially secular in their outlook. There is also deep factional rivalry among elites regarding the future direction of the country. These divisions were exacerbated as a result of the internal Iranian debate on the nuclear agreement. Elite conflict is also a precondition for a democratic transition. I would also add, there is a tradition of pro-democracy struggle in Iran that has shaped Iranian political culture. It is over a hundred years old and can be traced back to the 1905 Constitutional Revolution. (This tradition also includes the heroic efforts of Mohammad Mossadegh during the early 1950s.)

Unfortunately, the regional and international contexts have not been conducive to democracy. They have helped to bolster authoritarianism in Iran. The general chaos and instability in the Middle East, for which Iran has played a key role (especially in Syria), helps hard-line antidemocratic forces within Iran. The rise of ISIS and the broader Iran-Saudi rivalry, for example, allows the regime to exploit the theme of Iranian nationalism to rally people around the flag. In addition, this regional instability is exploited by Iranian leaders to scare people. They point to the chaos that could result from demands for political change along the lines of the Arab Spring. The Islamic Republic asks its citizens: Do you want Iran to be the next Libya, Yemen, or Syria?

Internationally, tensions with the United States are a key factor that inhibits democratization. Economic sanctions and threats of war generally bolster hard-line elements across most societies. Iran is no different here. Moreover, given the very troubled relations Iran has had with great powers going back to the 19th century, these interactions have deeply shaped Iranian political culture and resulted in deep sentiments of anti-imperialism. Iran's clerical leaders routinely exploit U.S. foreign policy machinations to shift attention away from their own failed policies and direct public attention externally by invoking themes of nationalism and anti-imperialism. In this sense, Trump has made the job of Iranian hard-liners much easier.

President Obama's Iran policy did provide a moment of hope and optimism for Iranian democratic forces. Many believed that a reduction in tensions, a growing economy, and greater global integration would create better social conditions for Iranians to organize and press forward with their democratic demands. There is still hope that this might be possible again if Trump loses in 2020.

Two final points on the prospects for democracy Iran.

As I've mentioned, the 2009 protests were mostly comprised of middle-class Iranians in urban settings; the 2019 protests were mostly Iranians of a lower economic status in the suburbs and smaller cities and towns. If these two groups revolt at the same time and for the same reasons, the Islamic Republic will be in deep trouble. What is also critical to a democratic transition in Iran is effective, courageous, and visionary leadership among opposition forces. This is currently in short supply.

The other potential flashpoint is the eventual passing of the supreme leader. He is the most powerful figure in the Islamic Republic. His inevitable death will produce a huge succession crisis that might create opportunities for democratic forces to exploit.

PART THREE
March 16, 2020

Can you discuss the significance of the killing of Qassem Soleimani by the United States and how this is related to the shooting down of the Ukrainian airline in Tehran in January 2020?

In early January 2020, the U.S. and Iran almost went to war. At the last moment, both sides de-escalated, but the prospects for a military confrontation remain very high. Here is the background.

In late December 2019, in response to U.S. sanctions and threats, an Iranian-backed militia in Iraq attacked a military base and killed an American contractor. The U.S. responded by targeting this militia group, killing over two dozen of its fighters. The U.S. embassy in Baghdad was attacked by supporters of the same Iraqi militia. Then, on January 3 (2020), in a surprise attack outside of Baghdad airport, an American drone killed Iran's top general, Qassem Soleimani. He was the architect of Iran's regional policy, with deep ties to Shi'a militia groups throughout the Middle East. Within Iran, he was portrayed as a war hero, due to his role in the Iran-Iraq

War and his efforts to defeat ISIS. In truth, he was a war criminal with lots of blood on his hands, especially in Syria, where was he involved with the Assad regime from the outset of the Syrian uprising in 2011 (when there was no ISIS/ Al Qaeda in the country).

Soleimani's assassination significantly raised the prospects for war. This would be the equivalent of Iran assassinating both the head of the CIA and the U.S. secretary of defense. Iran staged a massive funeral and vowed retaliation. A week later, Iran launched ballistic missiles at two U.S. military bases in Iraq. No one was killed, but more than a hundred American troops suffered brain injuries. Iran announced that if the U.S. were to retaliate by hitting targets on Iranian soil, Tehran would target Dubai and Tel Aviv. Thankfully, both sides pulled back from the brink after issuing mutual threats. In my view, had American troops been killed in this exchange, Trump would have likely retaliated against Iran, and there goes the Middle East. This is how close we came to a major regional war with huge global repercussions.

On the evening of the Iranian missile strike into Iraq (January 8), a Ukrainian passenger jet was shot down after leaving Tehran's main airport on a scheduled flight. More than 150 civilians were killed. For three days, Iran claimed it was a mechanical failure, but they were forced to admit that the IRGC accidentally shot down the plane during the fog of war. This produced renewed street protests, in part because of the regime's lies but also because many of the passengers on the plane were Iran's brightest students, who were traveling abroad to pursue their careers. To date, there has been zero accountability, and Iran refuses to hand over the black boxes to international aviation investigators.

How has Iran been affected by the coronavirus?

Iran was slow to react to this pandemic, and as a result, it has paid a huge price. [At this writing] after China and Italy, Iran ranks third in the world for the number of people who have contracted the virus and who have died as a result. Officially, the regime has acknowledged 700 deaths and 14,000 contaminations. Given the authoritarian nature of the regime, the real figure is certainly higher. On March 11, 2020, the *Washington Post* published satellite photos outside of Qum (one of the hardest-hit cities) that revealed mass graves the size of two football fields.

The Islamic Republic's response and management of the coronavirus crisis has been a total disaster. Iran's supreme leader, Ali Khamenei, came close to admitting culpability when he linked the low voter turnout during the February parliamentary elections to exaggerated fears of the virus outbreak. This clearly suggested that the focus of the regime was on shoring up its sagging legitimacy by encouraging a large voter turn-out, *not* in taking precautions to prevent this pandemic. He later advanced a conspiracy theory about a "biological attack" inflicted on Iran by its enemies. President Rouhani was more explicit. He described the coronavirus as "one of the plots and conspiracies that our enemies are pursuing."

What stands out is not only the large number of contaminations and deaths of average citizens, but how senior regime officials have contracted the virus. To date, senior ayatollahs, parliamentarians, vice presidents, and Khamenei's longtime foreign policy advisor, Ali Akbar Velayati, have been afflicted with the virus, and some have died. In a revealing event, Iran's deputy health minister appeared on television to reassure the nation that everything was under control. A day later it was announced that he had contracted the virus.

This is the third major self-generated crisis facing the Islamic Republic in recent months. The first was the November killings [during protests triggered by spiking fuel prices], and then there was the shooting down of the Ukrainian airliner, and now the COVID-19 pandemic.

The longer this coronavirus crisis lasts, the more it undermines the legitimacy of the Islamic Republic of Iran.

ABOUT THE AUTHOR

DAVID BARSAMIAN is founder and director of Alternative Radio (www.alternativeradio.org). His interviews appear in magazines and periodicals around the world. His latest books include *Global Discontents: Rising Threats to Democracy* (with Noam Chomsky) and *Culture and Resistance: Conversations with Edward Said.*

I Couldn't Even Imagine That They Would Kill Us
An Oral History of the Attacks Against the Students of
Ayotzinapa
By John Gibler, Foreword by Ariel Dorfman

Have Black Lives Ever Mattered?
By Mumia Abu-Jamal

The Meaning of Freedom
By Angela Y. Davis, Foreword by Robin D.G. Kelley

CITY LIGHTS BOOKS | OPEN MEDIA SERIES
Arm Yourself With Information